D0287957

TOWARD COMPREHENSIVE PEACE IN SOUTHEAST EUROPE

PREVENTIVE ACTION REPORTS
VOLUME 1

TOWARD COMPREHENSIVE PEACE IN SOUTHEAST EUROPE

CONFLICT PREVENTION IN THE SOUTH BALKANS

REPORT OF THE SOUTH BALKANS WORKING GROUP
OF THE COUNCIL ON FOREIGN RELATIONS
CENTER FOR PREVENTIVE ACTION

Edited by Barnett R. Rubin

Sponsored by the
COUNCIL ON FOREIGN RELATIONS
and the TWENTIETH CENTURY FUND

1996 ♦ THE TWENTIETH CENTURY FUND PRESS ♦ NEW YORK

DR
48.6
·C46
1996

THE TWENTIETH CENTURY FUND

The Twentieth Century Fund sponsors and supervises timely analyses of economic policy, foreign affairs, and domestic political issues. Not-for-profit and nonpartisan, the Fund was founded in 1919 and endowed by Edward A. Filene.

BOARD OF TRUSTEES OF THE TWENTIETH CENTURY FUND

Morris B. Abram	Lewis B. Kaden
H. Brandt Ayers	James A. Leach
Peter A. A. Berle	Richard C. Leone
Alan Brinkley	P. Michael Pitfield
José A. Cabranes	Richard Ravitch
Joseph A. Califano, Jr.	Arthur M. Schlesinger, Jr.
Alexander Morgan Capron	Harvey I. Sloane, M.D.
Hodding Carter III	Theodore C. Sorensen
Edward E. David, Jr.	James Tobin
Brewster C. Denny	David B. Truman
Charles V. Hamilton	Shirley Williams
August Heckscher	William Julius Wilson
Matina S. Horner	

Richard C. Leone, *President*

Library of Congress Cataloging-in-Publication Data

Center for Preventive Action. South Balkans Working Group.
    Toward comprehensive peace in southeast Europe : conflict prevention in the South Balkans : report of the South Balkans Working Group /edited by Barnett R. Rubin.
        p.   cm.
    Includes bibliographical references and index.
    ISBN 0-87078-402-1
    1. Balkan Peninsula--Politics and government--1989- 2. National security--Balkan Peninsula. 3. Yugoslav War. 1991- --Causes. 4. Yugoslav War. 1991--Peace. 5. Center for Preventive Action. South Balkans Working Group--History. I. Rubin, Barnett R. II Title.
    DR48.6.C46 1996
    949.702'4--DC20   96-27647
                                                                              CIP

OCLC#: 35285333   JUN 11 1997

COUNCIL ON FOREIGN RELATIONS

The Council on Foreign Relations, Inc. is a nonprofit and nonpartisan organization devoted to promoting improved understanding of international affairs through the free exchange of ideas. The Council takes no institutional position on policy issues and has no affiliation with the U.S. government.

From time to time, books, monographs, and reports written by members of the Council's research staff or others are published as a "Council on Foreign Relations Book." Any work bearing that designation is, in the judgment of the Committee on Studies of the Council's Board of Directors, a responsible treatment of a significant international topic. All statements of fact and expression of opinion contained in Council books are, however, the sole responsibility of the authors or signatories.

For further information about the Council or this report, please contact the Public Affairs Office, Council on Foreign Relations, 58 East 68th Street, New York, NY 10021.

Cover Design, Illustration, and Graphics: Claude Goodwin
Manufactured in the United States of America.
Copyright © 1996 by the Council on Foreign Relations. All rights reserved. No part of this publication may be reproduced, stored in a retrieval system, or transmitted, in any form or by any means, electronic, mechanical, photocopying, recording, now known, later developed or otherwise, without the prior written permission of the Council on Foreign Relations.

— NOTE —

The Council on Foreign Relations takes no position on issues. *Toward Comprehensive Peace in Southeast Europe* is a report of the South Balkans Working Group of the Center for Preventive Action (CPA), and the views expressed broadly represent those of the working group and the CPA Advisory Board. The report reflects the general policy thrust and judgments reached by the working group, although not all members of the group necessarily subscribe to every finding and recommendation in the report.

— ACKNOWLEDGMENTS —

This report was made possible by the generous support of the Carnegie Corporation of New York and the Twentieth Century Fund, Inc. The South Balkans Working Group is grateful to the authors; to Lori Fisler Damrosch and an anonymous reviewer for their helpful comments; to David L. Phillips, who organized the mission and carried out valuable research in Washington; and to Anya Schmemann, who supervised all administrative and production arrangements.

— CONTENTS —

— PREFACE —

THE CENTER FOR PREVENTIVE ACTION

The Center for Preventive Action (CPA) is a Council on Foreign Relations initiative to study and test conflict prevention—to learn whether and how preventive action can work by doing it. Many of today's most serious international problems—ethnic conflicts, failing states, and humanitarian disasters—could potentially be averted or ameliorated with effective early attention. Yet few have attempted to put this idea into practice, and even fewer have evaluated such attempts. The CPA uses the unique resources of the membership of the Council on Foreign Relations to fill these voids of action and understanding.

The primary function of the CPA is to learn about conflict prevention by engaging the members of the Council in such efforts. The CPA sends teams to pre-explosion crisis areas. These teams map out a strategy to settle or manage the conflicts and then advocate action by appropriate governments and organizations, national and international, private and public.

◆ An Advisory Board of Council members (see Appendix C), including diverse and experienced practitioners and experts, works in consultation with the CPA's professional staff to choose such pre-explosion areas of conflict for CPA action. The Advisory Board also assists in assembling the teams.

- The teams visit the area for approximately two weeks. There, they talk not only to politicians, but also to business leaders, religious leaders, journalists, nongovernmental organizations, and anyone else who can contribute to their understanding of the conflict. The group investigates both possible terms of a settlement and methods of bringing about a settlement by combining incentives, sanctions, and mediation.

Upon its return, the team presents a report or conceptual map of how to resolve or manage the conflict for review by the advisory group. The map is prepared in terms accessible to a wide policy audience. The CPA then publishes a report, briefs political and other leaders, writes articles and opinion pieces, and instigates congressional hearings and other actions. The CPA seeks to deploy the means at the command of the Council on Foreign Relations to mobilize the American and international communities to organize action to prevent conflict from escalating, or, better, to resolve it.

Subsidiary functions of the CPA include:

1. To convene an annual conference to assess the state of the art of conflict prevention. The conference brings together practitioners from governments, international organizations, and nongovernmental organizations (NGOs) with scholars, representatives of foundations, and Congress.

2. To serve as a coordinating center, letting everyone involved in conflict prevention know what everyone else is doing. In that regard, the CPA serves as a repository of relevant books, articles, and documents.

The Center for Preventive Action is funded by the Carnegie Corporation of New York, the Twentieth Century Fund, Inc. (for joint projects), the United States Institute of Peace, and the Winston Foundation.

THE SOUTH BALKANS WORKING GROUP

The South Balkans Working Group is chaired by Seymour Topping and consists of ten people who represent a variety of fields and areas of expertise. (See Appendix B for a complete list of members of and consultants to the working group.) The purpose of the working group is to recommend ways to prevent the spread of the ex-Yugoslav conflict into the South Balkans and to create a more enduring framework for peace and security in the region. (See map, page xii.) Members of the working group traveled to the region in early December 1995, and this report is based on the delegation's findings.

During the mission to the region, the delegation visited Belgrade (Serbia), Prishtina (Kosovo), Skopje, Tetovo, and Gostivar (Macedonia), and Tirana (Albania) where it met with many high-ranking officials, nongovernmental organizations, journalists, and community leaders. Among those whom the delegation met were Slobodan Milosevic, president of Serbia; Stojan Andov, acting president of Macedonia; Sali Berisha, president of Albania; and Bujar Bukoshi, prime minister of the autonomist government of Kosovo.

THE REPORT

The first part of this report presents an executive summary of the main findings and a list of recommendations. This part was written by Steven L. Burg and Barnett R. Rubin, with helpful comments from David L. Phillips. The second part, written by Burg, presents the historical background of the conflicts and recounts the process of fact-finding through which the working group arrived at its recommendations. Parts I and II broadly represent the views of the South Balkans Working Group.

In addition, we have included as Appendix A an article by working group member Victor A. Friedman, which gives further insight into the complex issues surrounding ethnic and other identities in the Balkans and also evaluates some previous efforts at conflict prevention by the international community. The views expressed in this section are those of Victor A. Friedman alone.

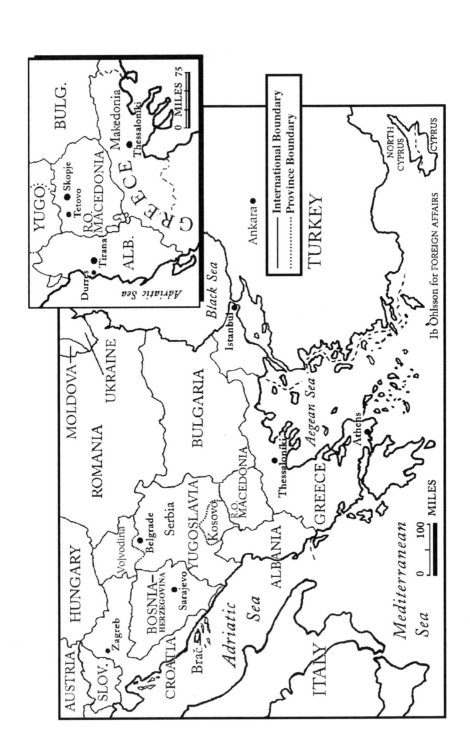

AUSTRIA
HUNGARY
SLOV.
● Zagreb
CROATIA
Brač
Vojvodina
BOSNIA–
HERZEGOVINA
● Sarajevo
● Belgrade
Serbia
YUGOSLAVIA
Adriatic
Sea
ALBANIA
Kosovo
R.O.
MACEDONIA
MOLDOVA
UKRAINE
ROMANIA
BULGARIA
● Thessaloniki
GREECE
● Athens
Aegean Sea
Black Sea
Istanbul
Ankara ●
TURKEY
NORTH
CYPRUS
CYPRUS

International Boundary
Province Boundary

Mediterranean
Sea

0   100
MILES

ITALY

Ib Ohlsson for FOREIGN AFFAIRS

YUGO.
BULG.
Tirana
Durrës
ALB.
Adriatic Sea
R.O.
MACEDONIA
● Skopje
Tetovo
Makedonia
● Thessaloniki
GREECE

0   MILES 75

— PART I —

POLICY RECOMMENDATIONS

STEVEN L. BURG

AND

BARNETT R. RUBIN

— 1 —

EXECUTIVE SUMMARY

The Dayton agreement on Bosnia-Herzegovina moves the troubled southeastern corner of Europe toward peace.[1] But we should not forget that many delayed for too long the actions needed to end the slaughter. As attention focuses on the difficult implementation of the agreement on Bosnia, we must not err again by neglecting other problems until they become violent conflicts. History will judge us harshly if we do not build on the achievement of Dayton to establish a comprehensive peace in the Balkans. Such a peace will require proactive initiatives to settle the conflicts that remain, particularly in the South Balkans, including Kosovo, Macedonia, and Albania.[2]

The dismemberment of Bosnia and the conflict in Croatia do not exhaust the list of dangers left by the breakup of Yugoslavia.

♦ The breakup of Yugoslavia arguably began in the province of Kosovo, where the ethnic Albanian majority (90 percent of the population) demands independence. The international community recognizes that Kosovo is a province of Serbia, but the Albanians of Kosovo (Kosovars) dispute this claim. Ignored at Dayton, the Kosovar leaders see the Bosnian Serbs gaining recognition as a result of violence, while their peaceful resistance goes unrewarded. Pressures are building for greater militancy.

◆ Neighboring Macedonia was economically devastated at the moment of its independence by the international embargo on its northern neighbor, Serbia, and a unilateral embargo imposed by its southern neighbor, Greece, which disputed the new republic's name and identity. The former embargo was ended by the Dayton accords and the latter by the interim agreement with Greece signed in September 1995, but the Republic of Macedonia is now struggling to rebuild, while its own restive Albanian minority (at least 23 percent of the population) raises demands that many ethnic Macedonians see as threatening their state's existence.

◆ Albania, Europe's poorest state and heir to its most repressive and closed communist regime, borders both Kosovo and the predominantly Albanian areas of Macedonia. Unrest or violence in either of its neighbors would menace that state's efforts to cast off the crushing burden of its past, an effort set back by the unfairly manipulated elections of May 27, 1996.

Outbreaks in Kosovo could quickly embroil Macedonia, as refugee flows and Albanian ethnic solidarity upset the precarious political equilibrium. Instability in Macedonia could send the entire political architecture of southeastern Europe crashing down. Nationalists in all of that country's neighbors—Serbia, Bulgaria, Greece, and Albania— have levied claims on its territory or denied its right to independent nationhood for more than a century.

Although these dangers are real, they are not inevitable, as a working group of the Council on Foreign Relations Center for Preventive Action found on a trip to the region during December 5–15, 1995. The Dayton agreement brought with it a new balance of power, and especially a new American engagement with the region, which has shaken up formerly rigid positions. Fear, mistrust, political manipulation, and nationalist passion may yet lead the South Balkans over the precipice, but some leaders on all sides, despite all the pull of their history, believe that after the Dayton agreement they can seek a different path. They differ on many points, but they agree on one: they cannot find that path alone. All, in one way or another, asked for international and, above all, U.S. leadership.

FRAMEWORK

In developing our recommendations, we were guided by one overall principle: stability here, as in the rest of Europe, must rest on implementation of the full package of Helsinki principles and commitments.

Much in the history of the region resists such principles. For a century or more the peoples of the Balkans have lived largely by the vision of nationalism, a vision they shared with much of the rest of Europe. Nationalism—the idea that humanity is divided into cultural groups called nations, which realize their values and destinies through independent statehood—inspired revolts against decaying empires and autocracies. Today the failure of Yugoslavia—itself an attempt to construct a state for five (later six) south Slavic nations—has further strengthened the nationalism of all its Slavic constituents as well as that of the other nationalities, such as Albanians and Hungarians.[3]

But a century of nationalism has failed the peoples of southeastern Europe, as it failed the rest of the continent as well. It brought pride at the cost of slaughter twice in this century in all of Europe, and a third time in the recent wars of the Yugoslav breakup. Out of this common past of national conflict, war, and genocide, the rest of Europe fashioned another vision, embodied in the Helsinki principles of 1975 and the Copenhagen documents of 1990, which established the "human dimension" as an integral element of security in Europe. That vision is one of respect for the territorial integrity of all states, but of states that permit free circulation of people and ideas: where states no longer fight over borders, because borders are channels of communication and exchange, not mere mechanisms of exclusion; where nations no longer fight for their own states, because their identities can flourish in free, plural societies; and where people need not look to exclusive identities for security, because states observe universal principles of human rights.

Such a vision may contradict the whole history of the Balkans, and weak, threatened nations such as the Albanians and Macedonians are the least likely to embrace it at once. But it offers the only alternative to a bloody past, and it is the region's only means to gain the security and ultimately the prosperity enjoyed by the rest of Europe.

RECOMMENDATIONS

With these principles in mind, we turn to specific recommendations for stabilizing the South Balkans.

GENERAL

◆ The United States should consider appointing a special envoy to deal with regional issues in the former Yugoslavia, including Kosovo; other ethnic issues in Serbia and Macedonia; and other questions not covered by the Dayton accords. Even in the absence of a special envoy, we urge intensified diplomacy—both quiet and public—in pursuit of an interim agreement in Kosovo and in support of new government initiatives to resolve interethnic tensions in Macedonia.

◆ To take maximum advantage of the influence that the international community (especially the United States) now has with Serbia, it is vital to maintain the so-called outer wall of sanctions against the Federal Republic of Yugoslavia until significant progress is made toward conflict resolution in Kosovo.[4] The Federal Republic of Yugoslavia, consisting of the republics of Serbia and Montenegro, has its own federal government but is largely dominated by Serbia and its president Slobodan Milosevic. (The Socialist Federal Republic of Yugoslavia, established by Marshal Josip Broz Tito, consisted of the same two republics plus Croatia, Bosnia-Herzegovina, Macedonia, and Slovenia, all of which are now independent states.)

MACEDONIA

The single most important action the United States can take to uphold Macedonian territorial integrity and security is to support continuation of the United Nations Preventive Deployment in Macedonia with U.S. participation until tensions in Kosovo have been reduced significantly. This force of Nordic and American troops (about 1,150 in total) monitors Macedonia's northern border.

The government of Macedonia, other governments, international organizations, and nongovernmental organizations should also cooperate to resolve Macedonia's ethnic and other problems in ways compatible with the vision of a pluralistic civic society. Our more detailed recommendations include expanded educational opportunities for ethnic Albanians, electoral reforms, augmentation of the powers of local governments, and continued improvement in bilateral relations between Albania and Macedonia.

Kosovo

Because the two sides are too far apart now to reach any agreement on the final status of Kosovo, we urge pursuit of an interim settlement that would defuse tension. The new situation that would then emerge might permit discussions that today seem impossible. We recommend a strategy with three stages, although we recognize they will not be fully distinct. These are

♦ Confidence-building measures

♦ Dialogue and negotiations

♦ An interim settlement

The most important confidence-building measures would be:

From Belgrade:

♦ Ending violations of human rights in Kosovo, including police repression, detention of political prisoners, and confiscation of passports;

♦ Assuring no repetition of the bans imposed in February on the operations of the Soros Yugoslavia Foundation and independent media, which have contributed to Serbian-Kosovar dialogue. The Soros Yugoslavia Foundation is the local foundation established by American philanthropist George Soros to support an open society in the FRY. It has aided independent media, publications, and dialogue;

♦ Permitting an increased international presence in Kosovo to monitor human rights, including reestablishing the mission of long duration of the Organization for Security and Cooperation in Europe (OSCE) and opening of offices by other international and nongovernmental organizations, as well as by foreign governments (information offices or consulates). We commend the opening of the United States Information Agency office in Kosovo on June 5, 1996, an event the Working Group helped bring about.

From the Kosovar leadership:

◆ Reaffirmation of the commitment to nonviolence;

◆ Reaffirmation and clarification of guarantees of the rights of the Serbian population of Kosovo, including international monitoring;

◆ Quiet communication of a willingness to defer discussion of independence while talks take place on interim measures to defuse tension.

From the international community:

◆ Pressing the Federal Republic of Yugoslavia (Serbia and Montenegro) to allow the OSCE to reopen its mission of long duration in Serbia.

◆ Establishing centers of operation in Kosovo by international humanitarian organizations such as the office of the UN High Commissioner for Refugees and the International Committee of the Red Cross, which now serve the region from other offices.

In the context of such confidence-building measures, international actors can use their good offices to assist communications and dialogue between Serbian authorities and Kosovar political leaders. Nongovernmental organizations should also seek to engage the parties, including nonofficial actors and social leaders, in a variety of dialogues.

These confidence-building measures and discussions should lead to an interim settlement that would relieve tension without requiring either side to renounce its firmly held positions on the final status of Kosovo. Such an interim settlement could include, for instance, agreement by Serbia to reopen and return to local control Albanian cultural and educational institutions in Kosovo and agreement by the Kosovars to participate in political institutions of the Federal Republic of Yugoslavia (although not those of Serbia).

In the long term, the entire Balkan region requires greater economic integration internally as well as with Europe if it is to grow and prosper. As a first step we recommend international financial and technical support for construction of an East-West transportation corridor through Macedonia that would link Bulgaria to Albania and its Adriatic ports. Other efforts at economic integration of the region and of the region into the rest of Europe should be encouraged.

— 2 —

RECOMMENDATIONS

The working group has developed several recommendations to promote stability and resolve interethnic tensions in the South
Balkans.[1] Our recommendations consist of both general principles and
specific measures to implement these principles.

In formulating these recommendations, the working group developed one guiding principle: *Uphold the full package of Helsinki norms as
they have evolved since 1989.*

Local actors often make references to "international norms" and to
"Helsinki principles" to legitimate their positions. Parties to disputes,
however, sometimes approach these principles selectively, citing those
that can be used to support their goals and practices and ignoring those
that may contradict their demands.

The right to self-determination cited by Albanian activists in both
Kosovo and Macedonia, for instance, does not necessarily constitute a
right to an independent state or territorial autonomy. Minority groups
are expected to exercise their rights through the institutions of the
existing state as long as those rights conform to Helsinki norms.
Similarly, state authorities cite the right of states to protect their territorial integrity. The Yugoslav government even argues that OSCE
principles obligate the Albanians of Kosovo to participate in state
institutions.[2] But the Federal Republic of Yugoslavia (FRY) has failed to

conform to Helsinki norms regarding even the most basic political rights of the Kosovar population.

The Macedonian government, while far more accommodating in its approach to its Albanian population, nonetheless appears not yet ready to adopt reforms that might eliminate cultural and political barriers to full participation by the ethnic Albanian population. In both Kosovo and Macedonia, although the situations are not comparable, suspicion and distrust with respect to the "real" ultimate goals of ethnic Albanian elites play a large part in fueling Serbian and Macedonian unwillingness to compromise.

Helsinki principles are thus often treated as if they were a menu of options. The working group concluded that the Helsinki principles as they have evolved since 1989 must be treated instead as a coherent package that imposes obligations as well as rights on all parties to these disputes. It is especially important for the international community to make absolutely clear its support for Macedonia as both a nation and a state, but to do so without seeming to exempt the government from its obligation to increase opportunities for democratic participation and national and cultural expression on the part of the Albanian minority (and others) in Macedonia.

Similarly, it is important for international recognition and economic support for the FRY to be linked to increased observance of Helsinki principles on the part of the Yugoslav regime. International actors must also convey to Albanian activists in Macedonia and Kosovo that Helsinki principles do not automatically grant a minority the right to an independent state, territorial autonomy, or recognition as a "constituent nation." Indeed, the principles that have emerged from the Helsinki process since 1989 focus on encouraging the development of democratic, civic states defined in terms of universal human rights, rather than nationalist states in which rights are linked to ethnic identities.

Strategically, the group concluded that Macedonia, Kosovo, and Albania constitute a common field of action that must be approached with a regional strategy. Stabilizing Macedonia is key to the entire region, but Kosovo is the factor most likely to destabilize Macedonia. Furthermore, a democratic, secure Albania eager to ensure its further integration with the rest of Europe and the West will be able to help resolve the conflict in Kosovo and promote interethnic coexistence in Macedonia. We begin with Kosovo, by far the most intense conflict in the region, and include a discussion of the role of Albania in finding a solution. We then discuss our proposals on Macedonia. Nevertheless we insist that all of the following recommendations be considered as a regional strategy that should be implemented together.

KOSOVO

There is an opportunity that should not be lost to reduce tensions in Kosovo. We recommend a strategy with three stages, although we recognize they will not be fully distinct. These are:

- Confidence-building measures

- Dialogue and negotiations

- An interim settlement

The interim settlement would create the "modus vivendi" that some of our interlocutors called for but would not require any of the actors to renounce their firmly held positions on the final status of Kosovo. Such an interim settlement could relieve much of the human suffering in Kosovo, help reintegrate the FRY into the international community, and ultimately create conditions for a future final settlement.

Implementing such measures will require a mixture of sanctions and incentives from the international community. The United States and its European allies should use the existing "outer wall of sanctions" against the FRY for leverage and their lifting as a reward for progress.

The remaining economic and political sanctions against the FRY have been gradually eroding in the wake of the Dayton agreement as some countries make individual decisions about their relations with Belgrade. Although ultimate reintegration of Serbia and the FRY is desirable, allowing the sanctions to erode without demonstrable progress on questions linked to preventing further conflict is shortsighted. Retaining these sanctions is *not an end in itself*. But the lifting of sanctions should be linked to clearly defined goals, including:

- Normalization of relations among all the successor states of the former Yugoslavia

- Full compliance with the Dayton agreement

- Cooperation with the International War Crimes Tribunal

- Implementation of confidence-building and normalizing measures in Kosovo

Implementing this strategy for Kosovo will require leadership by the United States. To assure that such leadership is exercised, the United States should appoint a senior official to have overall responsibility for implementing such a strategy. Finally, the United States and its partners should enlist the support of regional actors in this effort. Albania and Macedonia can be particularly helpful.

Confidence-Building Measures

An interim agreement must be approached with a great deal of sensitivity for the political constraints operating on both sides. It is imperative to increase the confidence of critical players on each side in the process of negotiation itself and in the possibility of a mutually agreed settlement. Each side must be convinced to undertake the *obligations* inherent in full implementation of international norms as a means of securing the *rights* embedded in them. The leadership on both sides must also be able to demonstrate to its followers that moving toward an interim agreement that does not satisfy maximal demands nonetheless provides concrete benefits. To build the confidence of each side in the good faith commitment of the other, extensive international monitoring of conditions in the province will be required. And, as incentives to comply, the international community must be prepared to reward compliance at each stage of the process.

To bring each side into compliance with international norms, such confidence-building measures would have to include the cessation of human rights violations in Kosovo, accompanied by the establishment of an international monitoring presence in the region. The former would encompass all dimensions of human rights and therefore permit the growth of civil society in Kosovo. It would include the release of political prisoners and the easing of passport and travel restrictions, as has occurred in recent months.

International monitoring represents an essential resource for verifying the compliance of each side for the other and for preventing extremists opposed to compromise from successfully employing misinformation to undermine popular confidence in the process. Restoration of the OSCE mission of long duration would establish such a presence, as well as clear an important obstacle to the reinstatement of Yugoslavia in the OSCE. Restoration and re-admission of the FRY to full membership in the OSCE should be made provisional and contingent on affirmation by an OSCE mission of compliance with OSCE human rights standards in Kosovo.

The above measures can be expected to increase the confidence of the Kosovar populace in their leadership and the confidence of the

Kosovar leadership in the good faith efforts of the Serbs. Similarly, the Kosovar leadership should be required to take measures that can be expected to increase confidence of the Serbian leadership in the Kosovars' good faith commitment to negotiating a solution. The Kosovar leadership should reaffirm its commitment to nonviolence and to protecting the equal rights of all residents of the province. The Kosovar leadership must make clear its willingness to defer demands for independence so as to make an interim agreement possible; it must also permit good faith negotiations to find a durable long-term solution.

DIALOGUE AND NEGOTIATIONS

The leadership of both sides says that it is ready for talks, but such talks are blocked by conflicting positions on modalities. Kosovar insistence on the presence of an international mediator and Serbian rejection of such an arrangement as an unwarranted "internationalization" of the problem seem to preclude official discussions at present. Therefore the role of bringing the two sides together might fall initially to nongovernmental organizations.

The goal of unofficial, second-track talks under unofficial auspices might be to generate ideas for confidence-building measures and the implementation of interim arrangements. Such meetings could also come up with ideas on how to break the deadlock over mediation or change the atmosphere so that some compromise on modalities becomes more acceptable.

AN INTERIM SETTLEMENT

Both Serbs and Kosovars suggested the idea of an interim settlement as a way to reduce tension without confronting the most difficult issues immediately. Final status issues would be left to a later stage, when relations among the parties might improve, as in the Israeli-Palestinian negotiations. Our interlocutors suggested that the elements of an interim settlement would be:

◆ Return of all Kosovo public institutions, including schools and the University of Prishtina, to normal operation

◆ Participation of the Albanian population in FRY (not Serbian) elections

◆ Conduct of these elections according to OSCE standards

The normalization of life in Kosovo would require the return to normal operation of all public institutions, including the return to work of the many individuals who were dismissed or who resigned from their jobs. The normalization of certain particularly sensitive institutions, such as the police and judicial institutions, might be carried out with the direct participation of international actors. All public institutions, however, would be subject to monitoring by the international actors present in the region. The educational system, including the University of Prishtina, should be returned to normal operation at the earliest possible moment.

Normalizing of local political institutions will present a particularly difficult challenge. FRY elections are now scheduled for 1997. The full participation of the Albanian population in those elections and the conduct of the elections according to OSCE standards (in Kosovo and the rest of Yugoslavia as well) could be established as a goal of the confidence-building and normalization measures. Such arrangements would address the immediate interests of both the Kosovars and the FRY. They might also permit the establishment of a process leading to a mutually agreed resolution in the long-term interests of both sides. It would be inappropriate for an outside actor to specify what that outcome should look like. It is appropriate, however, to suggest that the process might take the form of a constitutional reform by which the long-term status of Kosovo, and the structure of the Yugoslav state, might be redefined.

U.S. Leadership

Achieving agreement on the various elements of this strategy involves sensitive questions of sequencing. These might best be resolved by addressing all of them simultaneously or even by expanding the focus of OSCE action to include other former Yugoslav states. Success would require an agreement (or agreements) crafted with the same subtlety as was the September 1995 Interim Accord between Greece and Macedonia. It will also require the intensive diplomatic engagement of the United States.

The United States has already made clear its commitment to resolution of the Kosovo question. Secretary of State Warren Christopher stated in early February, after meeting with Serbian president Slobodan Milosevic in Belgrade, that the FRY "will never achieve full acceptance into the international community, will never achieve full approbation by the United States until it reconciles the status of Kosovo." He asserted that "Kosovo should have a status that will ensure respect for human and political rights of its citizens."[3] Assistant Secretary of State Richard Holbrooke, speaking two weeks later, reported that Kosovo is discussed in "every meeting with the Yugoslav leadership."[4]

Focused and sustained American leadership on issues identified in this report is essential. The Dayton experience demonstrates that such a focus is best achieved by designating a senior official with the appropriate authority to take charge of the issue. On some other issues, a special envoy has been appointed to fulfill this role. The appointment of such an envoy is, however, a sensitive matter. It automatically highlights an issue and raises expectations of both more direct American involvement and a quick solution. With respect to Kosovo and Macedonia, it may be premature to appoint a special envoy now. It is necessary, however, that the United States continue and even intensify its diplomacy—both quiet and public—in pursuit of an interim agreement in Kosovo and in support of new government initiatives to resolve interethnic tensions in Macedonia, as described below.

To ensure focused and sustained diplomatic efforts to achieve these goals, a senior official of the U.S. government should be assigned overall authority and responsibility for pursuing them, but for now this assignment should not be made a matter of public attention. This official should be responsible for dealing with all issues affecting progress toward resolving the ethnic problems in Kosovo and Macedonia. These issues would include, for example, seeking to assure the permanence of the June reversal of the February crackdown in the FRY on the independent media and on the efforts of the Soros Foundation of Yugoslavia to support the growth of civil society—a process essential to a durable, long-term peace.

The public designation of a special envoy, and the heightened American commitment and involvement it implies, should be reserved as a means to underscore the strength of American support for confidence-building measures and negotiations on an interim agreement in Kosovo, as well as measures to improve interethnic relations in Macedonia once some progress there is under way.

REGIONAL ACTORS

The United States should encourage and support efforts by Albania to secure peaceful resolution of the problems of Albanians in Kosovo and Macedonia while continuing to press the Albanian authorities to respect democratic norms internally. Resolution of the problems of ethnic Albanians in Kosovo and Macedonia clearly has domestic implications

for the leadership of Albania. A large part of Albanian leaders' motivation to support Western efforts appears to be based on their estimate of
the effect of progress in Kosovo and Macedonia on their own position in
Albanian politics. But an equally large part of their motivation lies in a
desire to strengthen their ties to the United States.

Both the FRY and Macedonia support the preservation of existing international borders out of self-interest. Albanian president Sali Berisha affirmed
this principle in direct talks with the working group's delegation to the region.
He has called repeatedly for external mediation between the Kosovars and the
authorities in Belgrade and has made it clear that Albania hopes to find a
peaceful solution to the dispute. "The Albanians of Kosovo cannot demand
less than the autonomy they enjoyed under the Yugoslav constitution of
1989," he said in an interview but added, "all changes made to borders by
force would mean a war option, while Albania and the Albanians of Kosovo
seek to avoid war."[5] The Albanian leadership's willingness to advise Kosovar
and Macedonian Albanian leaders to cooperate is an important resource.
Albanian support for the preservation of borders can play a critical role in
legitimating an eventual compromise by the Kosovar leadership. But
Albania will enjoy the stature needed to play this role only if it respects
democratic norms by, for instance, re-running last May's flawed elections and
assuring that September's municipal elections are indeed free and fair.

The United States should provide full support and encouragement
for the bilateral discussions now under way among Presidents Berisha of
Albania, Kiro Gligorov of Macedonia, and Milosevic of Serbia. It
should encourage and support the continuation of talks among Berisha,
Gligorov, and Ibrahim Rugova, leader of the Democratic League of
Kosovo and president of the unofficial "Republic of Kosova," as a means
to explore opportunities for further negotiation, mediation, or good
offices to resolve the Kosovo issue.

MACEDONIA

A strong, stable, democratic Macedonia is essential to stability in the
South Balkans. The single most important action the United States can
take to uphold Macedonian territorial integrity and security is to support
continuation of the United Nations Preventive Deployment in
Macedonia (UNPREDEP) with U.S. participation until there is significant progress toward reduction of tensions in Kosovo. Firm international commitment to the stability and territorial integrity of Macedonia
as signaled by UNPREDEP, consolidation of the Interim Accord with

Greece, and more general improvements in relations among all the states of the region will contribute to Macedonian stability.

Resolving tensions between ethnic Albanians and Macedonians as well as implementing measures for economic recovery are also crucial, however. We do not support binationalism, which would increase, rather than decrease, the saliency of national identity in politics. Instead we propose a set of measures that the Macedonian government can take to reduce the alienation of its ethnic Albanian population by moving in the direction of a civic definition of the state in which citizenship is defined less by ethnicity or nationality than by participation in public institutions with its concomitant rights and obligations. The United States should encourage and support efforts by the Macedonian government to implement such measures both through bilateral government-to-government relations and by supporting efforts by American and other nongovernmental organizations to help Macedonian citizens strengthen civil society.

A few key international efforts can make important contributions to stability in Macedonia. First, the United States should support continuation of UNPREDEP. The soldiers of UNPREDEP, about 650 Nordic and 550 American, helped stabilize Macedonia in the difficult years of the Greek blockade. Their presence on Macedonia's border with Serbia signaled international determination to contain or halt violence in Kosovo. Some believe that the signal they send of international and, above all, U.S. commitment to Macedonia's territorial integrity continues to have a calming effect on the country's domestic ethnic problems.

Furthermore, to protect the resources necessary to meet social needs, the Macedonian government must limit military expenditures. UNPREDEP reduces the pressure on the Macedonian government to divert valuable resources from the civilian to the military sectors. Expansion of the North Atlantic Treaty Organization's Partnership for Peace in the region (Macedonia and Albania have already joined) should include efforts to minimize military expenditures on the part of the Balkan states by securing a balance of forces among them at the lowest possible levels.

Second, the United States should support economic recovery in Macedonia. No effort to reduce ethnic conflict is likely to succeed in Macedonia if economic and social conditions deteriorate. In the long term, the entire Balkan region requires greater economic integration internally as well as with the rest of Europe if it is to grow and prosper. As a first step we recommend international financial and technical support for construction of an East-West transportation corridor through Macedonia that would link Bulgaria to Albania and its Adriatic ports. This route through Macedonia, already under discussion, would complement the existing North-South route linking Serbia to Greece and its ports. Other efforts at economic integration of the region and of the region into the rest of Europe should be encouraged.

Next we turn to internal reforms. Although internal reforms are above all the responsibility of the government and citizens of Macedonia, international support for these efforts will be vital. Such support should come partly from friendly governments, but in most cases nongovernmental organizations will be most effective in providing assistance in the task of building a democratic civil society.

We found two key areas where reforms could make a difference: education and the political system. Access to public sector employment and opportunities in the private sector and privatization programs are also important, and we include a few remarks on these subjects.

In education we in general recommend measures intended to transform nationalist demands into demands for quality education by legalizing the university in Tetovo as a private institution, establishing procedures for accrediting private institutions of higher education, increasing opportunities for Albanian-language instruction in state institutions of higher education, and improving the quality of secondary education in languages other than Macedonian, including Albanian.

In government and politics we recommend measures designed to encourage pluralism within and between ethnic communities and to enable politicians to deliver concrete benefits to constituents by equalizing the population of electoral districts across the country, introducing a measure of proportional representation into the legislative electoral system, and strengthening the autonomous powers of local government over taxation, delivery of services, and language use.

EDUCATION

There is an extraordinary level of mobilization around the university in Tetovo issue among ethnic Albanians. Ethnic Albanians established an unofficial Albanian-language university in the city of Tetovo in February 1995. The Macedonian authorities regard this university as illegal, and one Albanian youth died in demonstrations at its founding. Albanians insist that they founded the university to meet genuine educational needs, while Macedonians generally regard it as a political initiative aimed at introducing separatist Albanian institutions as in

Kosovo. Helsinki principles clearly protect the right of individuals to found independent educational institutions, though the government may regulate their accreditation. To deescalate interethnic conflict— or, at least, deny an important issue to extreme nationalists—the Macedonian government should end its opposition to the university in Tetovo. The government might consider treating it simply as a private institution. That would signal an end to the Communist practice of treating nonstate initiatives as subversive and a move toward a model of a civic state in accord with Helsinki principles.

For this approach to work, the government would have to develop and apply an agreed accreditation process to all institutions of higher education. Such accreditation should be in the hands of an officially authorized but autonomous professional body. For at least an interim period, such a body might work in collaboration with an advisory group of international experts, which could be assembled, for instance, by the relevant bodies of the OSCE.

To ensure further that legalization of the university does not encourage disintegration and "parallelism" as feared, the government would simultaneously have to expand the domain of Albanian-language instruction at Skopje University (including its Bitola campus). The choice for Albanian students must not be between the university in Tetovo or no education, but between Tetovo and the opportunity to pursue a quality education in Skopje or Bitola. If the government can convert the competition between the state-funded school and the private university into a competition based on the quality and effectiveness of the education students will receive, Macedonia cannot lose.

Because Macedonian fears about the cultural survival of their nation contribute to interethnic and international tensions, it is important not to permit outside involvement in Macedonian development to become, or to be perceived as, one-sided support of Albanian cultural demands. The United States should therefore accompany efforts to facilitate the satisfaction of Albanian cultural needs with efforts to support Macedonian cultural development.

If the Macedonian government redefines the frame of reference for higher education issues, it can transform the question into how to deliver the best education. Considerable international expertise in curriculum development and university management, expert knowledge of education in bilingual and multicultural settings, and practical experience in the organization and operation of systems of accreditation can be brought to bear on this issue. Specific goals can be set with respect to ethnic composition of enrollments, instruction in Albanian and

Macedonian, faculty composition, and other quantifiable aspects of university operations (after expert review of current conditions). International experts can provide continuing evaluation of successes and shortcomings in meeting specific goals.

The participation of international educational professionals rather than diplomats in goal-setting activity can help depoliticize these issues and professionalize the decision-making processes by which goals are pursued. Such goal-setting and evaluative activities can and should be carried out in cooperation with local experts as part of the strategy of substituting professionalization for politicization in this area. Sharing responsibility for evaluation with external experts contributes to objectivity and, therefore, to local confidence in the results.

By expanding, diversifying, and improving instruction, including technical education, at the secondary school level for Albanian-language speakers, the Macedonian government can both improve the qualifications and ability of Albanian-speakers who attend Skopje University and moderate the demand for higher education by promoting practical career alternatives. The government might also consider expanding opportunities for Macedonian-speakers to learn the Albanian language as a means of moving toward bilingualism as a norm for future generations of elites.

PUBLIC SECTOR EMPLOYMENT AND PRIVATIZATION

A similar strategy can be applied to resolving disputes over employment in the public sector. The delegation heard several conflicting statistical summaries of and arguments about the ethnic composition of public sector employment. The Macedonian government should permit international experts to conduct periodic verifications of its data on the ethnic composition of public sector employees to ensure their accuracy. The government might also seek expert assistance in devising programs to redress imbalances in the patterns of employment including, perhaps, movement toward a policy of bilingualism in the public sector. Any such program, however, must incorporate a long period of transition. In the interim, the government must continue to implement its policy of affirmative action.

In the long run, economic progress in Macedonia will depend on the growth of the private sector. In western Macedonia the working group delegation observed a boom in housing construction, as ethnic Albanians repatriated cash they had earned either in the West or in other parts of the former Yugoslavia (many had owned hotels and restaurants on the

Dalmatian coast, for instance). In Gostivar the delegation lunched in Benny's Pizza, a restaurant run by a dynamic Albanian entrepreneur who seems to have learned the art of making thin-crust pizza in Texas. As the economy recovers from the blockade and sanctions, international institutions should work with their Macedonian counterparts to ensure that these entrepreneurial skills are put to work in service to the economy of the country. Privatization should not be limited to those who already have access to the state sector.

GOVERNMENT AND POLITICS

Our interviews suggest that electoral reform should be designed to equalize the population of electoral districts and introduce some element of proportionality in the distribution of seats. Such reforms can contribute to the pluralization of politics within the ethnic Albanian community. The probable increase and diversification of ethnic Albanian participation in parliament that would result from such changes would create additional opportunities for ethnic Albanian representatives to participate in coalition politics and to influence government policies.

Careful attention must be paid to the internal organization of parliament to improve its effectiveness as an arena for the early resolution of ethnic issues. The description of the parliamentary Council for Inter-Ethnic Relations provided to the delegation by then-Acting President Stojan Andov suggested that it could play a greater role in giving minority populations an effective voice in government.[6] Expanded and more effective representation can do much to legitimate the Macedonian political order within the ethnic Albanian community.

Both governmental and nongovernmental actors can provide important expertise and practical assistance in reforming Macedonia's electoral system and parliamentary procedures. Western nongovernmental agencies with considerable expertise in the organization of political parties and the conduct of elections are already on the ground in Macedonia. The delegation, for instance, had a useful discussion with the local representative of the National Democratic Institute for International Affairs.

On the basis of the delegation's experience, however, it is not clear whether those preparing the electoral reform in Macedonia are making use of the considerable expertise in other countries concerning the probable impact on interethnic relations of differing choices regarding districting, balloting, rules of representation, and other aspects of the electoral system. For example, although it is clear that some form of proportionality is to be introduced in Macedonia, there are many different definitions of proportionality and ways it might be achieved. Similarly, parliamentary procedure appears to be guided largely by the rudimentary rules laid out in the constitution. The development of more specific rules and procedures is an area in which there is considerable international expertise. The Council of Europe, OSCE, and the European Parliament all offer institutionalized expertise in these matters. Western scholars have devoted considerable attention to the impact of electoral and parliamentary decision rules on interethnic conflict.

The United States and international organizations should also allocate resources to help support efforts to strengthen local government in Macedonia. The proposed legislation on local self-government that was under consideration during our stay in Macedonia did not appear to satisfy local leaders' wishes for authority and resources to meet the needs of their constituents. By expanding local leaders' ability to address the real needs of the population, the Macedonian government may be able to deescalate conflict over the larger state. To depoliticize ethnicity at the local level, the government might build on the local traditions of ethnic tolerance, described to the delegation, by permitting the use of minority languages in the conduct of local business in state offices.

CONCLUSION

Complex as this strategy is, our experiences during the mission and the reactions to our proposals since then have convinced us that the opportunity for action is real. Recent incidents of violence show that the danger is real: in April, two Albanians (including a thirteen-year-old boy) and five Serbs met violent deaths in Kosovo, and in June unknown gunmen killed one Serb policeman and wounded two others. It is up to the United States and its allies to use these opportunities to avert yet more violence and move toward a comprehensive peace in the Balkans.

— PART II —

SUPPORTING MATERIAL

Steven L. Burg

— 3 —

STABILIZING THE SOUTH BALKANS

The South Balkans is a region beset by insecurities. Conflicts with the potential to destabilize the region and to draw NATO or other states into the fray remain unresolved. The most urgent of these is the situation in the southern Serbian province of Kosovo, where the leadership of the local majority population of ethnic Albanians has maintained a strategy of nonviolent resistance in the face of extensive Serbian and Yugoslav government repression. The longer this confrontation remains unresolved, the greater the threat that it will turn violent. The status of Kosovo and the demands of its Albanian populace are embedded in the larger ethnic Albanian question in the southern Balkans. That question involves not only the Federal Republic of Yugoslavia (Serbia and Montenegro), referred to as FRY, but Macedonia and Albania as well.

Macedonia represents the linchpin of stability in the southern Balkans. Historically, Macedonia has been the object of territorial ambitions on the part of all its neighbors. Any threat of instability in Macedonia, and especially any threat to the territorial integrity of the country, raises the prospect that the ambitions of its neighbors and the inevitable international conflicts they would engender might be revived. The challenge to the Macedonian government of normalizing its relations with its neighbors is compounded by the task of resolving internal tensions between its ethnically Macedonian and Albanian populations. Developments in neighboring Kosovo have had a direct, destabilizing effect on ethnic relations in Macedonia. Hence, the stability of Macedonia depends to a significant degree on the peaceful resolution of the situation in Kosovo.

Developments in Kosovo also affect and are affected by the domestic and international politics of Albania. Neither the unrest in Kosovo nor the tensions in Macedonia can be resolved in isolation from each other or from developments in Albania. Stabilization of the South Balkans will therefore require coordinated efforts to settle the problems in Kosovo and Macedonia, to neutralize both the Kosovo and the Macedonia questions in Albanian domestic politics, and to normalize relations among Albania, Macedonia, the FRY, Bulgaria, and Greece.

The United States has important interests at stake in the region. The long-term success of the Dayton agreement may depend on resolving ethnic problems in the FRY, including Kosovo. In the case of Kosovo, the Bush and Clinton administrations have committed the United States to opposing any further crackdown by Serbia on the Albanian population. In December 1992, President George Bush, in a letter to Serbian president Slobodan Milosevic, stated that, "in the event of conflict in Kosovo caused by Serbian action, the United States will be prepared to employ military force against the Serbs in Kosovo and in Serbia proper."[1] Although this statement does not commit the U.S. government to act, any president is likely to come under significant pressure from domestic constituencies to fulfill this apparent pledge to use force in the event of violent conflict in the province.

U.S. troops provide nearly half of the United Nations' Preventive Deployment (UNPREDEP) force stationed in Macedonia. These 500 U.S. troops represent a clear and visible signal of the American commitment to Macedonian territorial integrity. Although UNPREDEP directly protects Macedonia against some external threats to its integrity, it may alleviate internal sources of instability only indirectly. Foremost among these are the ethnic tensions in the republic. Were conflict in Kosovo to lead to secessionist efforts among Macedonia's Albanians, UNPREDEP would be faced with a new and politically more difficult challenge to the territorial integrity of the state it is deployed to defend. Hence, the success of U.S. commitments in both Kosovo and Macedonia requires efforts to resolve ethnic tensions.

Alleviating the external and internal threats to Macedonian stability, and especially the links between them, will require careful action by many local and international actors, both official and unofficial, and may seem daunting. The working group carried out an extensive schedule of formal interviews and meetings, as well as informal contacts, in the region in December 1995, and in February 1996 Steven L. Burg, consultant to the working group, held follow-up discussions in the FRY. These revealed a new political dynamic. The Dayton agreement has provoked local actors to reconsider their options and has created an opportunity to achieve progress on all three sides of the triangular dynamic of stability in Albania, Kosovo (FRY), and Macedonia.

The next section provides background information on the interethnic tensions in Macedonia and Kosovo and describes the dynamics of these situations in the period leading up to the Dayton accords. The subsequent section describes what the delegation learned about the various forces at play in Kosovo, Macedonia, and Albania and, especially, about the apparent impact of the Dayton agreement on the stakes and opportunities perceived by local actors.[2] The report identifies what these findings suggest in terms of opportunities to alleviate tensions in the region and to help move the parties toward peaceful resolution of their conflicts. These findings form the basis for the recommendations presented in Part I.

HISTORICAL BACKGROUND

Instability in the South Balkans has both international and domestic sources. The legacy of historical competition among several Balkan nations for control over Macedonian territory and the desire of Albanians in several states for some form of independence or unity contribute to international instability. The domestic sources of instability are to be found in the inherent difficulties of accommodating competing claims to status and power by multiple, mobilized ethnic groups in a single state and in the difficulties of moderating nationalist aspirations once they are ignited. Interethnic tensions inside Macedonia are also magnified by the dispute between ethnic Albanians and Serbs over the neighboring province of Kosovo. That dispute directly affects the attitudes, goals, and behaviors of both ethnic Albanians and ethnic Macedonians in Macedonia in ways that make resolution of the tensions between them more difficult.

THE KOSOVO PROBLEM

Nationalist discontent has been prominent among the ethnic Albanians of Kosovo since 1968, when the first large-scale demonstrations in the history of Communist Yugoslavia broke out.[3] The 1968 events were characterized by extreme hostility between ethnic Albanians on one side and Serbs, Montenegrins, and Macedonians on the other. Ethnic Albanian demonstrators raised demands for national self-determination, for separation from Yugoslavia, and for union with neighboring Albania. One of the more moderate demands was for elevation of the status of the province to that of a full-fledged federal republic.[4] Serbs viewed this demand with suspicion: Kosovo was an autonomous province within the Serbian republic. Because republics enjoyed the formal constitutional right to self-determination, the demand for elevation to republic status was viewed as a stepping-stone to secession.

Most of Kosovo has been part of Serbia since the Treaty of Bucharest of 1913. The territory that makes up what is now Kosovo was ceded to Serbia following the defeat of the Ottoman Empire in the first Balkan War (1912–13). The Serbian claim to the region reflected the historical attachment of the Serbs to lands they view as the "cradle" of the Serbian nation: the Serbian Orthodox Church was founded at Pec, in western Kosovo, and the defeat of a Serbian army by the Ottomans in Kosovo Polje in 1389 remains a defining element in Serbia's nationalist narrative. The border between Albania on one side and Serbia and Macedonia on the other was finally fixed in 1921, when territories disputed by Albania and Yugoslavia were divided between them. The border has not changed since (except for the Italian occupation during World War II). Ethnic Albanians make their own similar historical and political claims to the region. Kosovar Albanians often point out, for example, that the nineteenth-century national awakening among ethnic Albanians was centered in Prizren, in southwestern Kosovo.[5]

Over time, the ethnodemographic character of the region has changed from ethnically mixed to overwhelmingly Albanian. In 1948 Serbs constituted 23.6 percent of the population, while ethnic Albanians were 68.5 percent, proportions that remained relatively stable until 1961. By 1971 rapid population growth among the Albanian population had begun to shift the ethnic balance in the region. Albanians constituted 73.7 percent of the population in 1971 and 77.4 percent in 1981.[6] No accurate count of the ethnic Albanian population was possible in 1991, when the Albanian population boycotted the census, but Yugoslav statisticians estimated that 82.2 percent was ethnic Albanian.[7] Rexhep

Ismajli, an Albanian intellectual, estimates the Albanian proportion of the population in 1991 as 90 percent, a figure that does not seem unreasonable in light of the massive outmigration of Serbs that occurred after 1981 as a result of rising ethnic tensions in the region.[8]

With the devolution of power to the republics and provinces in federal Yugoslavia in the early 1970s, a largely ethnic Albanian leadership emerged in Kosovo. This leadership was dedicated to advancing regional and ethnic Albanian interests. Operating within the constraints imposed by the still-strong military-security control over the province exercised by Belgrade, the leadership of Kosovo expanded Albanian cultural institutions and widened contacts with neighboring Albania. Albanian-language higher education and cultural life gradually slipped out of the hands of the communist elite and into those of more nationalist intellectuals. Prishtina University became a hotbed of political activism driven by discontent with the social and economic underdevelopment of the province and growing nationalist aspirations.

These burst forth in 1981 in another round of nationalist demonstrations, accompanied by renewed calls for republic status for Kosovo within the Yugoslav federation, as well as for outright unification with Albania. The 1981 demonstrations were put down with a brutal display of force that alienated the ethnic Albanian population still further. This repression set off a series of violent confrontations between the Albanian population and the Serbian state. Relations between ethnic Albanians and the local Serb population of Kosovo worsened, leading to an acceleration of the outmigration of Serbs from the province and an increase in police repression of the ethnic Albanian population. Throughout the 1980s Albanian-Serb relations worsened. Resentment of the loss of control over Kosovo contributed to the rise of a Serbian nationalist backlash in Yugoslav politics.

Rising Serbian nationalism in the late 1980s accelerated the destabilization of Yugoslavia, becoming the vehicle for the seizure of power in Serbia by Slobodan Milosevic and leading to increased Serbian repression of the Kosovars.[9] A series of amendments to the Serbian constitution adopted in March 1989, followed by a new constitution adopted in September 1990, eliminated the autonomy of the provinces. This change was carried out against the background of enormous pressure against Kosovo, which led to a new round of resistance to Serb control. In July 1990 115 ethnic Albanian members of the provincial parliament declared the independence of Kosovo. These deputies had been elected in December 1989 but had been prevented from working by the Serbian authorities.

The 1990 declaration of independence prompted a severe crack-down. Serbian authorities closed the provincial parliament, took over the provincial government, ended Albanian-language instruction at the University of Prishtina, and intensified political repression. In September 1990, an alternative Kosovar Albanian leadership proclaimed a "Constitution of the Republic of Kosova." In September 1991 the alternative leadership organized an extralegal referendum in the province, in which the overwhelming majority of the ethnic Albanian population participated, declaring its support for independence. This referendum was followed by a formal declaration of the independent "Republic of Kosova" in October and the beginning of a popular boycott of official Serbian institutions.

Despite Serbian repression, or perhaps because of it, the number of political parties and groups in Kosovo proliferated in the late 1980s. The most important of these was, and is, the Democratic League of Kosova (LDK), which was conceived from its beginning as a broad, national movement. It was led by Ibrahim Rugova, the president of the Writers' Association. In May 1992 extralegal, multiparty elections were held to establish a new parliament and government for the region. At the same time Rugova ran unopposed for president. The newly elected alternative leadership of Kosova embarked on an effort to build a network of alternative social institutions independent of Serbian control. To a very large extent, they have succeeded.

At present, Kosovo is characterized by a military-political stalemate. An extremely well-armed Serbian security force of 30,000 armored and mechanized security troops and 65,000 reservists provides a formidable deterrent to any violent uprising on the part of the Albanian population. At the same time, all political legitimacy and popular authority among the ethnic Albanian population of the region rests in the hands of the Rugova government.

Since 1981 Macedonia has provided a form of "escape valve" for Kosovars fleeing repression. Large numbers of Kosovar refugees seem to have settled in Macedonia, while others have passed through Macedonia on their way out to employment or sanctuary elsewhere and on their way back to Kosovo.[10] The presence of numerous refugees from Kosovo among the ethnic Albanians of Macedonia strengthens the already strong ties between these two populations. Until Serbian authorities closed it in 1990, the University of Prishtina in Kosovo had provided the main source of higher education for Macedonia's Albanians. Thus, large numbers of Macedonian Albanian students were exposed to the same social and political influences as their peers in

Kosovo, who formed the backbone of the Albanian nationalist move-ment there. Much of the content of those influences, in turn, was shaped in Communist Albania, which supplied faculty and instruc-tional materials to Kosovo. The closure of the University of Prishtina has contributed to the pressure in Macedonia to expand higher educa-tional opportunities in the Albanian language.

The political leaderships of the Kosovar, Montenegrin, and Macedonian Albanians have explicitly attempted to coordinate their positions through the Council of Albanian Political Parties in the Former Yugoslavia.[11] Established in 1991 under the leadership of President Rugova, the Council declared at the outset that any change in the internal borders of the former Yugoslavia would open the door to the demand that other Albanian-populated territories—including those in Macedonia—be unified with Kosovo. In the event of secession by other republics, the Albanian lands would insist on union with Albania.[12] Thus there is ample precedent to expect that a partition of Bosnia-Herzegovina would increase demands for separation among eth-nic Albanians.

MACEDONIA

The contemporary state of Macedonia is the creation of the Yugoslav Communist regime. The Yugoslav Communists created the Macedonian republic as a constituent unit of the Yugoslav federation to fulfill the national aspirations of the Macedonians, as well as to oppose the claims of Bulgarians, Greeks, Serbs and, later, Albanians to this territory. Both the history of regional competition for control over Macedonia and the denial of a distinct Macedonian identity by those who sought to control that territory affect contemporary Macedonian political behavior. Bulgarian, Greek, and Serbian nation-alism and resistance to Ottoman rule fueled the several Balkan wars of the late nineteenth and early twentieth centuries. The territory that is now the Macedonian state passed from Ottoman to Serbian control as a result of these wars. It became part of Serbia in 1913 and, there-fore, part of the first Yugoslavia in 1918. It was subjected to Albanian and Bulgarian occupation during World War II but reverted to Yugoslavia afterward. The boundaries of the contemporary Macedonian state correspond to those established after World War II by the Communists, which approximate those established for the first Yugoslavia. These borders remained essentially unchanged throughout the Communist regime.

Macedonia, like the other federal republics of the former Yugoslavia, enjoyed extensive political autonomy under the Communists. It was ruled by the League of Communists of Macedonia, a suborganization of the federally organized League of Communists of Yugoslavia. The republic's party was dominated by ethnic Macedonians.[13] The Macedonian party led local efforts to strengthen a distinctive Macedonian national identity through the republic's political, educational, and cultural institutions. The Macedonian state was defined constitutionally during the Communist period as "the national state of the Macedonian people, and the state of the Albanian and Turkish nationalities in it, based on the sovereignty of the people." The constitution affirmed that members of other groups who lived in the republic enjoyed legal equality and had the same rights and obligations as Macedonians, Albanians, and Turks.[14] The Macedonian state was thus defined as both a national, or ethnic, state, and a civic one. As in Bosnia-Herzegovina, however, these definitions were in inherent conflict with one another.

Macedonian identity was (and still is), for Macedonian-speaking Slavs, both ethnic and political, or civic, in nature. For Macedonians, there is no contradiction between these definitions of the state. For ethnic Albanians and other, less numerous non-Macedonian groups, however, the ability of the Macedonian state to command their loyalty depends heavily on the degree to which the civic definition of the state, with its emphasis on legal equality, outweighs the ethnic one in determining public policies and practices. The Communist-era constitutional distinction between "nations" (Macedonians) and "nationalities" (Albanians and Turks) corresponded to a clear difference in political status. The former represented a privileged category; the latter, a category subject to de facto, if not de jure, discrimination. Discrimination against ethnic Albanians became especially pronounced in Macedonia after the 1981 outbreak of unrest in Kosovo and the subsequent attempt by the Communist regime to repress all manifestations of ethnic Albanian nationalism.

For ethnic Albanians the attraction of an ethnic alternative to Macedonian civic identity, whether of a more localized ethnic or larger Albanian nationalist variety, is reinforced by the history of discrimination in Yugoslavia and by what ethnic Albanians perceive as the continuation of inferior status in the postcommunist state. The postcommunist constitution also defines the state, in its preamble, as the "national state of the Macedonian people" based on "the historical, cultural, spiritual and statehood heritage of the Macedonian people and their struggle over centuries for national and social freedom, as well as for the creation of their own state."[15] Only then does it concede "full equality as citizens and permanent coexistence with the Macedonian people" to Albanians, Turks, Vlahs, Romanies, and other nationalities. This distinction between nation and nationality preserves the separation maintained under the Communists between these two categories. As in the former Yugoslavia, it suggests the inferior political status of the latter.

In the body of the Macedonian constitution itself, the ethnic, cultural, and linguistic identity of national minorities is guaranteed in a number of instances. But several apparent contradictions and omissions have become the foci of political dispute. Article 7 of the constitution defines Macedonian as the official state language. This declaration is moderated by the stipulation that nationalities may use their own language in local affairs where they constitute a majority or "a considerable number" of the inhabitants.

Articles 8 and 48 establish the freedom to express one's national identity as well as the right to establish institutions through which to do so. This includes the right to primary and secondary education in one's own language. In such schools, however, Macedonian must also be taught. The constitution is silent with respect to the language of instruction in institutions of higher education. It also gives citizens the right to establish private schools above the level of primary education.

Opposition to the definition of the state articulated in the preamble was evident from the outset. Albanian members of the Sobranie (the Macedonian parliament) boycotted the vote to adopt the constitution in November 1991. The small Serb minority in Macedonia, which constituted only 2.2 percent of the population in 1991, protested the fact that it was not granted explicit minority status. Serbian extremists, including the notorious Vojislav Seselj, attempted unsuccessfully to exploit discontent among the Serbs to destabilize Macedonia in 1992 and 1993 in much the same way they destabilized Bosnia-Herzegovina.[16]

The ethnic dimension of Macedonian state identity was also a source of political conflict on the international level. A constitutional provision affirming that the state "cares for the status and rights of those persons belonging to the Macedonian people in neighboring countries" helped to fuel a dispute with Greece, where the government and much of public opinion interpreted the provision as an expression of territorial ambitions against Greek Macedonia—this even though the Greek constitution itself contains a similar provision in article 108, stipulating that the Greek government "shall care for

Greeks residing abroad and for the maintenance of their ties with the Motherland." The constitutional provision, plus Greek opposition to Macedonian claims to the name Macedonia itself and to the use of the star of Vergina as a national symbol, were used to justify Greece's opposition to recognition of the republic by the European Community (EC) and the imposition by Greece of an embargo on the republic. Thus, the ethnic Macedonian character of the emerging state engendered both internal and external opposition.

Confronted in early 1991 with the imminent disintegration of the Yugoslav state, Macedonia's leaders joined the Bosnian Muslims in an attempt to bring about agreement on the creation of a loose federation among the republics. That effort failed, leaving both the Bosnians and the Macedonians with few political options. The onset of fighting in Slovenia and Croatia, the de facto support of the international community for dissolution of Yugoslavia along existing republic borders (manifest in the July 1991 Brioni agreement that ended the fighting in Slovenia), and the movement toward recognition of republics that declared their independence (evident in the pronouncements of the EC and the proposals of its Conference on Yugoslavia in September and October 1991), impelled the reluctant Macedonians (as well as the Bosnians) toward independence.

After conducting a successful referendum on independence in September, the republic leadership declared Macedonian sovereignty and, in November 1991, independence. Unlike Bosnia, however, Macedonia was not drawn into war. Like Slovenia, and unlike Bosnia (or Croatia) there was no significant historical Serb irredenta in Macedonia whose population could wage civil war against the state or attract support from Serbia. (The Serbs of Macedonia could, however, still provide a pretext for intervention by extreme Serb nationalists.) Thus, the Yugoslav Peoples' Army (*Jugoslovenska Narodna Armija*) withdrew peacefully from the republic in April 1992, taking or destroying its weaponry and equipment, leaving the defenseless Macedonian state with only a small, poorly equipped military. Macedonia was also heavily dependent on relations with Serbia for its economic well-being.

Insecurity about Macedonian borders is reinforced by the living memories among Macedonians of the Bulgarian and Albanian occupations of these territories during World War II and by the contradictory characteristics of current relations with Albania and Bulgaria. That both Bulgarian and Albanian foreign policies combine elements of support for Macedonia with opposition to the concept of an ethnic Macedonian nation preserves suspicions in Macedonia and abroad that these states continue to harbor territorial ambitions toward their neighbor. Bulgaria was the first state to recognize Macedonia, although only as a state, in January 1992. Bulgarian nationalists regard the Macedonian language as a mere dialect of Bulgarian, and Bulgaria's stubborn avoidance of recognizing or legitimating the existence of a distinct Macedonian ethnic identity has caused some difficulty in bilateral relations. But the overall good relations, including extensive economic relations, between the two states have greatly reduced the likelihood of international conflict on Macedonia's eastern border. Relations with Albania, in contrast, have remained uncertain as a result of the support shown by some Albanian officials for the more radical ethnic Albanian leadership inside Macedonia. Macedonian insecurity is reinforced as well by the historical memory of Serbian expansion earlier in this century and the threat that contemporary Serbian nationalist extremists might seek to expand Serb control southward.

Fighting elsewhere in the former Yugoslavia and the continuing tensions between ethnic Albanians and Serbs in neighboring Kosovo led some actors, domestic and international, to fear a spillover of violence into Macedonia, further heightening the insecurity of the new state. This fear led directly to the decision to send the United Nations' first preventive military deployment to Macedonia in December 1992. The simultaneous dispute with neighboring Greece over the name, symbols, and apparent ethnoterritorial ambitions of the Macedonian state meant that Macedonia enjoyed good relations and secure borders with only one of its four neighbors. Even in the case of Bulgaria, however, a proposal to establish open borders between the two states could be seen as both stabilizing and destabilizing. To pressure Macedonia to concede on the issues in dispute, Greece imposed a severely damaging trade blockade against it in 1992 and closed its border with Macedonia in 1994.

The problems posed by these relationships were magnified by the delay on the part of Western states in extending diplomatic recognition and support to Macedonia following the collapse of Yugoslavia. This delay stemmed from the efforts of Greece to block such recognition. The Arbitration Commission, established as part of the EC Conference on Yugoslavia, had decided in January 1992 that Macedonia had met all conditions for diplomatic recognition by the EC. But the EC failed to act because its consensual decisionmaking practices allowed Greece to block any action. Delay of the collective decision also delayed recognition by individual member states.

The ability of Greece to block recognition began to fade in spring 1993 as European states grew impatient with Greek intransigence in the face of conciliatory efforts by Macedonia that included the adoption of constitutional amendments specifically disavowing territorial ambitions or interference in the internal affairs of other states.[17] The Europeans increasingly worried about the potential spread of the conflict in Bosnia-Herzegovina. To sidestep Greek objections to the use of the name Macedonia, European members of the UN Security Council forged a compromise formulation allowing Macedonia to be admitted to the United Nations under the name "Former Yugoslav Republic of Macedonia" in April 1993. The resolution admitting Macedonia also mandated Macedonian-Greek negotiations to resolve outstanding issues. Adoption of this compromise did not come without cost to the Macedonian government, however. It engendered considerable domestic resistance. The parliament passed the measure by a narrow margin, with thirty in favor and twenty-eight opposed. There were thirteen abstentions, and forty-nine deputies elected not to be present for the vote. Less than a week later, the Macedonian nationalist opposition party, the Internal Macedonian Revolutionary Organization (VMRO, in its Macedonian acronym), called for a no-confidence vote, which failed.[18]

Admission to the United Nations opened the door to wider diplomatic recognition. Albania, apparently under pressure from Turkey, recognized Macedonia the same month.[19] Belgium extended diplomatic recognition in October 1993, followed by Denmark, France, Germany, the Netherlands, and the United Kingdom in December. The United States extended recognition in February 1994, although it withheld establishing full diplomatic relations in deference to the continuing Greek embargo. Russia, however, recognized the state under the name "Republic of Macedonia." Recognition was widely seen in the West as a means to prevent the spread of fighting and as a necessary step toward stabilizing the internal politics of Macedonia itself.

Increasing Western support for the new state came in direct opposition to the rising tide of nationalism and hostility toward Macedonia in Greece. Elections in Greece in fall 1993 brought to power a government committed to a hard-line approach to relations with Macedonia. The government of Andreas Papandreou refused to participate in face-to-face negotiations mediated by UN envoy Cyrus Vance and closed the Greek-Macedonian border in February 1994. Refusal to recognize Macedonia was, however, a costly policy for Greece. Macedonian territory encompasses the most direct overland transportation routes for Greece's commerce with its European partners. The present UN sanctions against Yugoslavia aside, it was contrary to Greek economic interests to alienate Macedonia and contribute to the degradation of the Macedonian infrastructure. In addition, the Greek port of Thessaloniki represented Macedonia's closest point of access to the international economy. The Greek blockade shut down an obvious opportunity for economic growth for both countries. Moreover, closing the border gave further impetus to the redirection of trade from the north-south route through Thessaloniki to the East-West route from the Albanian port city of Durres to Istanbul, through Macedonia and Bulgaria. Finally, Greek intransigence on this issue contributed to its growing isolation and loss of influence in the European Community.

Negotiations continued in the form of proximity talks. In February 1994, the United States appointed a special representative to assist in the talks. Despite all the rational economic and political reasons why Greece should have been willing to negotiate a solution to this dispute sooner rather than later, it still required a final push from the United States and a subtly crafted document to convince Greece to sign the agreement negotiated by UN envoy Vance and his deputy, Ambassador Herbert Okun, together with U.S. envoy Matthew Nimetz.

The interim accord signed at the United Nations on September 13, 1995, addressed most Greek concerns. It called for further negotiations to resolve remaining issues, and, most important for Macedonian development, it formally ended the economic blockade. Following this agreement, Macedonia was admitted to the Organization for Security and Cooperation in Europe (OSCE) and, more recently, to the Council of Europe. International recognition has also unblocked Macedonian access to financial help from international institutions such as the International Monetary Fund and World Bank.

With the establishment of international diplomatic and economic relations and the negotiation of a solution to the dispute with Greece, the external threats to Macedonian security have narrowed significantly. Several problems remain unresolved, however. The border with Greece is not yet fully open. Relations with Bulgaria remain unclear. But the two most pressing issues remain relations with Yugoslavia and Albania.

To prevent the conflicts in Croatia, Bosnia-Herzegovina, or Kosovo from spilling into Macedonia and to secure Macedonia against more direct aggression by Yugoslavia (Serbia), Macedonian president Kiro Gligorov requested in November 1992 that the United Nations deploy observers to the republic. This request was supported, if not actually initiated, by Vance and Lord David Owen, cochairs of the International Conference on the Former Yugoslavia (ICFY). In early December, after having sent a fact-finding mission to the republic, UN secretary general Boutros Boutros-Ghali recommended such deployment to the Security Council, which authorized it by the adoption of Resolution 795 (December 11, 1992).[20] The initial deployment took place in January 1993, when about 150 Canadian troops arrived. These were replaced by a Nordic battalion of about 650 troops in March. In July 1993, 300 U.S. troops were added to the force, and another 250 were deployed in spring 1994. Because a clear, agreed international border has not been established between Yugoslavia and Macedonia, UN forces negotiated a military administrative border between them, which helped to control border incidents between Yugoslav and Macedonian forces. The OSCE sent several fact-finding missions and established a long-term mission to Macedonia in September 1992.[21] These efforts also focused on monitoring borders and preventing spillover.

The most important factor in reducing tensions, however, has been the physical presence of international forces, and especially U.S. troops, along the Macedonian-Yugoslav and Macedonian-Albanian borders. They create an effective deterrent to any open assault against Macedonia from either Yugoslavia (Serbia) or Albania. In March 1995 the UN secretary general reported that there was "no current military threat" to the country.[22] In January 1996 the primary outstanding international issue reported by the secretary general remained the need to negotiate mutual recognition and the normalization of relations between Macedonia and the FRY.[23] That finally took place on April 8, 1996, when the FRY and Macedonia officially established diplomatic relations.[24]

The presence of such troops does not, however, foreclose the possibility that an outbreak of fighting in Kosovo might spill into Macedonia. And while their presence contributes to reducing tensions in their areas of operation, it does not resolve the fundamental challenge of achieving a political agreement that stabilizes interethnic relations in the republic. As events in Bosnia have demonstrated, international peacekeepers would be of little assistance in the event of internal war between ethnic groups.

Efforts focused more directly on resolving domestic conflicts in Macedonia have been carried out by the High Commissioner on National Minorities (HCNM) of the OSCE, former Dutch foreign minister Max van der Stoel, who has made several trips to Macedonia. In November 1993 van der Stoel responded to increasing conflict over educational policies between the ethnic Albanian minority and the government by recommending that the government accelerate efforts to accommodate Albanian demands. He also recommended that the government strengthen the role of the Council of Inter-Ethnic Relations provided for in the constitution.[25] Van der Stoel also was present in Macedonia in February 1995, when ethnic Albanians attempting to establish their own Albanian-language university in Tetovo clashed with Macedonian police, resulting in many injuries and one death. The HCNM called for "restraint" and "for all the parties to remain calm." He suggested that the issue of Albanian-language instruction at the university level be dealt with in the framework of a new law on higher education.[26] Van der Stoel's recommendations reflect his general approach to conflict resolution, which emphasizes direct negotiation and decisionmaking through recognized institutional procedures.[27] Public documents do not suggest, however, the nature of the solution van der Stoel may have had in mind.

International mediators, working first in the context of the working group on national minorities of the EC Conference on Yugoslavia, then in the context of a working group of the successor organization, the ICFY, and finally as part of the Office of the High Representative, Carl Bildt, have carried out a continuous effort to mediate conflicts between the government and ethnic minorities.[28] They have attempted to formulate specific recommendations for institutional and procedural reforms by which to resolve intergroup conflicts. It has been reported, for example, that as long ago as February 1993 mediators facilitated agreement between the Macedonian and ethnic Albanian leaderships on constitutional changes designed to alleviate intergroup tensions. Failure to implement the agreement was attributed to the fact that the government and ethnic Albanian parties did not command between them the necessary two-thirds majority in parliament to secure passage of a constitutional amendment.[29]

Mediators have achieved other successes in moderating conflict between the government and smaller ethnic groups, including the Serbs of Macedonia. But their efforts have not yet narrowed the differences between ethnic Albanians and Macedonians on such key issues as language policies—including the use of Albanian in higher educational institutions—and local self-government. Nor do they appear to have addressed other areas in which intergroup conflict might be deescalated: electoral and parliamentary reforms.

The ability of mediators to bring the parties together for intensive discussion of the educational and language issues represents an important factor favorable to their solution. However, the long-term involvement of the same mediators in a series of intergroup conflicts in the former Yugoslavia produced a tendency to apply variations of the same power-sharing formula to each of these conflicts, even though such formulas have failed to attract support from the conflicting parties themselves. Macedonia may provide an appropriate opportunity to reconsider these principles and to devise new ones. And it may provide an appropriate opportunity to consider electoral and parliamentary reforms as a means to deescalate conflict.

The ethnic problem in Macedonia differs in important ways from that in Kosovo. Politics in Macedonia is far more openly pluralistic than in Kosovo. Several political parties compete for support in the ethnic Albanian community in Macedonia. Two Albanian parties are represented in parliament (along with other Albanians who are independent or affiliated with a nonethnic party). One Albanian party participates in the government coalition, which is led by the Social Democratic Alliance of Macedonia (SDSM, in its Macedonian acronym), a nonethnic, or civic, party. Albanian political parties participate in local (*opstina*-level) government in areas with large ethnic Albanian populations. The government in the Tetovo region, for example, includes representatives of both an Albanian and a Macedonian party, and the government in Gostivar is entirely Albanian. Albanians thus play an important role in the domestic politics of Macedonia. The most important Albanian parties at present are the Party of Democratic Prosperity (PDP in English, but PPD—*Partia per Prosperitet Demokratik*—in Albanian), a party that appears to be torn between participation in government and opposition, and the PPD-Sh (*Partia per Prosperitet Demokratik-Shqiptare*, or Party of Democratic Prosperity-Albanian), formed by a more radically nationalist group that split off from the PPD. (Table 3.1 shows the distribution of seats in the Macedonian parliament.)

Although there have been several confrontations, and some Albanian actors report being victimized by political persecution, ethnic Albanians in Macedonia are not subject to repression as are ethnic Albanians in Kosovo. They do, however, object to a series of government actions and policies that they view as discriminatory. These include government policies on the use of Albanian in official (government) business, the status of Albanian as a language of instruction at the university level, the status of the university in Tetovo founded by Albanians, access to employment in state institutions for ethnic Albanians, the degree of autonomy granted to *opstina*-level governments, and the perceived inequalities in the election laws. All the ethnic-Albanian parties and factions are pressing for greater cultural equality, for expanded local self-government and, ultimately, for the establishment of what amounts to a binational state in which the Albanian population would be elevated constitutionally to a status equal to that of the Macedonian nation. Some more moderate Albanian politicians still hope to establish a civic state and a political system based on nonethnic parties.

The political dispute between ethnic Albanians and the Macedonian state includes even the most basic question: how many ethnic Albanians are there in Macedonia? Census data alone rarely reflect the complexities of self-identification in any diverse society. In Macedonia, they fail to capture the complex relationships among religion, language, ethnicity, and politics that define individual choices about national identity. The Albanian-language population of Macedonia is divided by religious and racial or ethnic cleavages, as is the Macedonian-language community. No ethnic group defined by these cleavages can be assumed to be politically homogeneous. Ethnic groups in Macedonia are internally divided between radicals and moderates, between confrontationists and cooperationists, and between state builders and secessionists. Even where one political party appears to command the support of the overwhelming majority of a group, as the PPD does among ethnic Albanians, that party is characterized by deep internal differences.

Censuses can record the relative size of groups. The 1991 census, however, conducted as Yugoslavia was collapsing, was boycotted by the ethnic Albanian community, whose political leaders claimed their

TABLE 3.1
1994 MACEDONIAN ELECTIONS
DISTRIBUTION OF PARLIAMENTARY SEATS

PARTY	NUMBER OF SEATS
Alliance for Macedonia (coalition)	
Social Democratic Alliance of Macedonia (SDSM)	58
Liberal Party (LP)	29
Socialist Party (SP)	8
Party of Democratic Prosperity (PPD)	10
Democratic People's Party (PDP)	4
Other small parties and independents	11

Note: Due to a government shakeup in February 1996, the Alliance for Macedonia coalition and the composition of the Council of Ministers have changed since the time of the delegation's visit.

Source: Duncan M. Perry, "On the Road to Stability—or Destruction?" *Transition* (August 25, 1995), p. 43.

community would be purposefully undercounted. As a result, the number of Albanians recorded in the census was determined through a process of statistical estimation carried out by Macedonian authorities (see Table 3.2).[30] Ethnic Albanian political leaders refused to accept the number—441,987, or 21.7 percent of the total population—arrived at by the authorities.[31] Some insisted that ethnic Albanians constituted as much as 40 percent of the population, or 700,000 to 800,000 people. (See map, page 46.) Several other minorities also claimed to have been undercounted. When added together, the population claims of all minorities following the 1991 census far exceeded the total population of the republic. As Victor Friedman concludes in the most detailed study of the census question in Macedonia to date, "These claims clearly sacrificed statistical accuracy to an effort to gain political power and hegemony."[32]

The completion of an extraordinary census conducted in 1994 by international authorities did not resolve these disputes. As the table presented below demonstrates, that census basically affirmed the absolute and relative sizes of ethnic groups reported in the 1991 data. But, as Friedman argues, the manner in which it was carried out, and even the fact that it was carried out at all, probably intensified the conflict between ethnic Albanians and Macedonians rather than moderating it.[33] Indeed, despite the apparent accuracy of the 1994 effort, Albanian leaders have resumed claiming that their community was undercounted.

Claims by ethnic Albanian leaders that the ethnic Albanian population of the country has been undercounted reinforce their demands for greater participation in public institutions and for constitutional recognition as a "constituent nation" of the Macedonian state. They reject the status of "nationality" or "minority" and demand constitutional recognition as a "nation" and re-definition of the Macedonian state as the state of both the Macedonian and the Albanian nations. The Macedonian leadership, however, rejects all such proposals for constitutional change.

TABLE 3.2
NATIONAL COMPOSITION OF THE POPULATION OF MACEDONIA, 1991 AND 1994

	1991		1994[a]		1994[b]	
	NUMBER	**PERCENT**	**NUMBER**	**PERCENT**	**NUMBER**	**PERCENT**
Macedonians	1,328,187	65.3	1,378,687	66.4	1,288,330	66.5
Albanians	441,987	21.7	478,967	23.1	442,914	22.9
Turks	77,080	3.8	81,615	3.9	77,252	4.0
Roms	52,103	2.6	47,408	2.3	43,732	2.3
Serbs	42,775	2.1	39,866	1.9	39,260	2.0
Others	91,832	4.5	48,653	2.4	45,389	2.2
TOTAL	2,033,964	100.0	2,075,196	100.0	1,936,877	100.0

Notes:
a 1994 population calculated according to 1991 counting rules (persons living abroad for more than one year are included, but persons resident in the country for less than one year, refugees, persons under humanitarian care, and others are excluded).

b 1994 population calculated according to 1994 counting rules (includes all persons with legal residence in the country, persons temporarily resident for at least one year, persons with legal residence in the country but abroad for not more than one year, persons employed abroad, and their families; excludes refugees and persons under humanitarian care).

Source: Soopstenie 1: Popis '94: Podatoci za Segasnosta i Idninata, Prvi Rezultati (Communication 1: Census '94: Data for the Present and the Future, First Results) (Skopje: Republicki Zavod za Statistika, 1994), pp. 3, 4, 28.

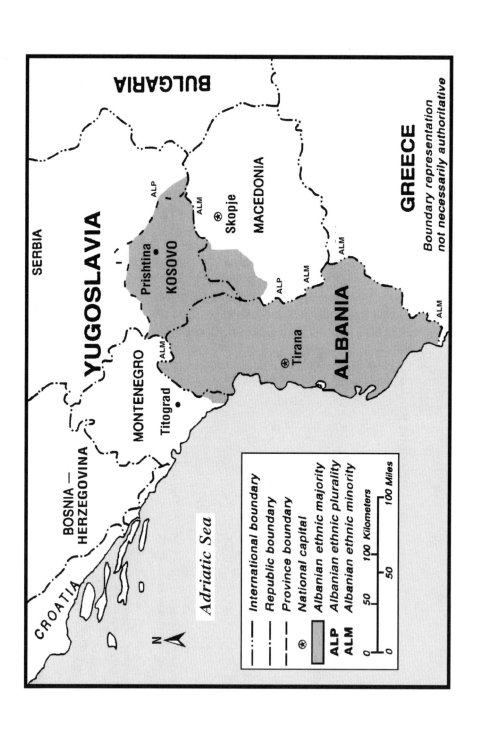

BULGARIA

SERBIA

YUGOSLAVIA

MACEDONIA

GREECE

Boundary representation
not necessarily authoritative

KOSOVO

Prishtina

ALP

ALM

Skopje

ALP

ALM

ALM

ALM

ALM

MONTENEGRO

Titograd

Tirana

ALBANIA

BOSNIA —
HERZEGOVINA

CROATIA

Adriatic Sea

N

International boundary
Republic boundary
Province boundary
National capital
Albanian ethnic majority
Albanian ethnic plurality
Albanian ethnic minority

ALP   Albanian ethnic plurality
ALM   Albanian ethnic minority

0   50   100 Kilometers

0   50   100 Miles

— 4 —

THE FIELD MISSION

The delegation of the working group on the South Balkans visited Belgrade (capital of Serbia and the Federal Republic of Yugoslavia), Prishtina (provincial capital of Kosovo), Skopje (capital of Macedonia), Tetovo and Gostivar (Albanian majority districts in western Macedonia), and Tirana (capital of Albania) in December 1995. In Belgrade the delegation heard two distinctly different approaches to the Kosovo problem. From government officials, the delegation heard an uncompromising demand for Kosovars to end their boycott of Serbian and Yugoslav institutions. From some others, however, the delegation heard a clear acknowledgment that the situation in Kosovo had reached a deadlock and that new initiatives were required. The mission heard the suggestion that Kosovo be granted "the maximum autonomy possible" as a means of reaching an interim agreement that would normalize conditions in the province and permit negotiations that might lead to a longer-term settlement of the problem.

The delegation received further encouragement from some views expressed by Kosovar leaders. When speaking in their official capacities, Kosovar Albanian leaders voiced only their uncompromising demands for internationally mediated negotiations with Serbia leading to full independence for Kosovo. But some Kosovar leaders privately showed a new flexibility with respect to the process by which a solution might be found. While not relinquishing their commitment to eventual independence, some Kosovar leaders also acknowledged interest in reaching an interim agreement with Belgrade that would permit normalization of conditions in Kosovo and the conduct of further negotiations over a longer-term solution.

The similarity between some views in Belgrade and some views among Kosovar leaders suggests that an interim settlement of the Kosovo problem might be reached through negotiations between the Kosovars and the Serbs. The delegation's meetings in Tirana with Albanian president Sali Berisha suggested that such a strategy would enjoy important additional support from Albania.

It was clear to the delegation after its visit to Macedonia that tensions between the ethnic Albanian population and the Macedonian government represent a serious challenge to stabilizing that country. The delegation found, however, that the problem in Macedonia is very different from that in Kosovo. The ethnic Albanian population of Macedonia is not being subjected to repression. In a series of interviews with ethnic Albanian political leaders, the delegation identified several areas of perceived discrimination and inequality that contribute to political discontent. The most important issue fueling interethnic tensions in Macedonia today is the unresolved status of the university established in Tetovo by ethnic Albanians. The Tetovo university issue, in turn, is closely linked to the question of Albanian-language instruction at Skopje University, which has become even more key since Serbia terminated Albanian-language instruction at the University of Prishtina. The character and status of the university in Tetovo and the scope of Albanian-language instruction at Skopje University are extremely divisive issues that must be resolved soon in a manner that contributes to the deescalation of tensions.

Other issues, including electoral reform, the strengthening of local self-government, public employment policies, and language usage in public institutions, are also sources of intergroup tensions. But these are questions that can be addressed by government action. The delegation's interviews with leading government officials suggest that the Macedonian government is committed to addressing them in a constructive manner. The government, however, which consists of a coalition of Macedonian and ethnic Albanian moderates, faces significant challenges from both Macedonian and ethnic Albanian nationalists advocating more extreme measures. The Macedonian government must therefore construct responses to these issues that strengthen moderate forces in both the ethnic Albanian and the Macedonian communities. The ultimate aim is to strengthen civil society so that ethnic identity is no longer linked to the state, the central object of political struggle, but becomes part of civil society. Private organizations specializing in education, interethnic relations, and other areas of institution building can play an important role supporting such developments.

BELGRADE

The delegation began its mission in Belgrade where it met with Serbian officials, influential individuals, and journalistic observers of the local political scene to discuss the situation in Kosovo and possible means for resolving it peacefully. The decades-long conflict between Serbs and ethnic Albanians over the status of Kosovo has resulted in wide-ranging, well-documented Serbian repression. The Serbian authorities have carried out a campaign of persistent police repression, including physical abuse, against the Albanian population of Kosovo. Repression has extended to the suppression of educational, public health and cultural institutions and, of course, genuinely representative local government. Repression has not increased popular compliance with the Serbian regime, but peaceful resistance has not broken the determination of that regime to control the province. The overwhelming military force available to the regime and its apparent willingness to use it make violent resistance impractical. The present situation has all the characteristics of a political deadlock between Serbia and the leaders of the Democratic League of Kosova (LDK). The latter constitute a genuine national leadership, having come to power as a result of alternative elections held in May 1992, and have established themselves as an alternative "government of the Republic of Kosova."

Some activist groups and political figures in the West have expressed sympathy for LDK demands for independence for Kosovo. The publicly articulated position of the LDK allows for no result short of this. But formal international approaches to the Kosovo problem have recognized that the region is a part of Serbia and, therefore, the Federal Republic of Yugoslavia (FRY). Moreover, Serbia has employed an overwhelming level of force to ensure that any attempt by the Kosovars to establish their independence unilaterally can be suppressed. Although the FRY leadership has participated in the past in discussions of the situation held under international auspices (that is, the working group on national minorities of the International Conference on the Former Yugoslavia), the leadership's current position is that the Kosovo question is a strictly internal issue. Any solution will therefore have to reconcile these seemingly mutually exclusive, publicly articulated positions.

During its discussions in Belgrade, the delegation heard both the formal, uncompromising position of official Belgrade and more nuanced and pragmatic views. The latter offered hope that some progress toward a negotiated solution is possible. The most extensive statement of these views was heard during our meeting at the Institute for International Politics and Economics (*Institut za Medjunarodnu Politiku i Privredu*— IMPP).

The delegation met with a group of academics and journalists led by the director of the institute, Dr. Pedrag Simic. Simic outlined what he defined as a possible approach to a negotiated solution. He conceded at the outset that Serbia must be prepared to negotiate the maximum degree of autonomy possible, but within the framework of the FRY. It should be noted that he did not insist that that autonomy be established within the framework of Serbia. He acknowledged that this solution might not necessarily satisfy the Kosovar Albanians, but he claimed that there was a willingness on the Serbian side "to work this out politically." He pointed to experience outside Yugoslavia as the source for possible models and specifically mentioned the South Tyrol, one of several examples of regional autonomy that the institute has researched and analyzed.[1] The South Tyrol was also mentioned by others during our visit to Belgrade, suggesting that this idea may be one that is already circulating rather widely. The South Tyrol "model" consists of extensive local self-administration, full linguistic equality within the province (although Italian remains the "official" state language), educational and cultural autonomy, and proportionality in public employment. A key element in the establishment of the South Tyrol solution was the willingness of the Austrian state to encourage and support compromise between the local German-speaking population and the Italian state.[2]

Simic expressed the desire to find what he called a modus vivendi with the Kosovars for the short term. He argued that as much as one year of talks might be required to find such a modus vivendi. This, he argued, would then permit continuing talks to reach agreement on a lasting solution. The latter, he suggested, might then be implemented over five to ten years.

Simic's remarks reflected an important realization on the part of at least some Serbian actors: that it is necessary to start a process of genuine discussion to build mutual confidence and understanding between

Serbian and Kosovar leaders. The specific outcome of such talks cannot be stated in advance. Thus, neither side would be compelled to renounce its publicly articulated position in advance. Simic suggested that such an approach might create a significant opportunity for the two sides to "find a solution together."

Our discussions at the IMPP also revealed, however, that such an approach would give rise to conflicts among the Serbs. A representative of the Foreign Ministry who attended the discussion (M. Pajic, chief of the North American department) felt compelled, for example, to contradict the flexibility shown by other participants and to reinforce less conciliatory official positions. We met this official again during our visit to the ministry the next day. The IMPP discussion also made clear that efforts to resolve the Kosovo issue that call for greater autonomy for the province may be used by some Serbs as leverage to demand greater autonomy for the Republika Srpska (the Serbian entity that, together with the Muslim-Croat Federation, constitutes Bosnia-Herzegovina under the Dayton accord) and thereby further the partition of Bosnia.

The vast majority of those in the room for our IMPP meeting remained silent. This was not because of a language barrier, since two members of the delegation spoke Serbo-Croatian. It seemed to reflect more the sensitivity of the issue and, perhaps, a certain degree of tension surrounding our visit. One of the most provocative observations during our meeting was offered by a Serbian specialist in Latin American issues who has in the past shown a sensitive understanding of what is on the minds of policymakers. She reflected the fear among Serbs that no compromise could satisfy Albanian ambitions when she observed that Kosovo and Albania were like *spojni sudovi* (connected vessels, or a jug with two spouts) and that both worked toward a "greater Albania" solution. This was an example of a widely held Serbian view. Later, in Albania, the delegation heard a more complex perspective on this relationship. At the IMPP, this comment produced animated support in the room. Despite this fear, this individual made it clear during a private aside that preceded the group discussion that she welcomed our visit as a sign that the isolation she and her colleagues had been feeling was coming to an end. She welcomed our effort to encourage a peaceful settlement of the Kosovo conflict.

The views expressed at the IMPP were echoed by Dragoljub Micunovic of the Democratic Center, an independent organization devoted to supporting democratization and the peaceful resolution of conflict in the FRY. The delegation also heard such views, somewhat surprisingly, from Vuk Draskovic, the leader of the Serbian Renewal

Movement and otherwise well-known as an advocate of Serb nation-alism. Such views can be taken as a reflection of the thinking among a small, but serious group of Belgrade intellectuals and are consistent with Micunovic's personal efforts to foster intergroup dialogue and achieve a peaceful solution. The views expressed by Draskovic may reflect little more than political tactics. That Draskovic feels compelled to take such positions, however, reflects the impact of the Dayton agree-ment on political thinking in the region: more local actors, including even Serbian nationalist actors, perceive both the need and the oppor-tunity to negotiate solutions to ethnic conflicts. The role of the United States is central to such thinking. Those actors who contemplate inter-national participation in negotiations see the United States as a nec-essary partner in such processes.

A certain degree of pragmatism also was evident among Serbian guests at a dinner held at the U.S. ambassador's residence. Fragmentary informal discussions with Belgrade-based democratic activists before dinner made clear their desire for a negotiated settlement. This was not surprising. But these discussions also suggested a hesitancy about whether such talks were, in fact, possible.

One individual with extensive personal involvement in grassroots democratic activities in Kosovo suggested that the delegation try to learn about these activities and intimated that there is a wider range of political views among Kosovars than those represented by the LDK. This view was reinforced in a later, longer, and more detailed conver-sation in the United States with a prominent and well-informed Serbian democratic activist, who reported on the activities of several independent, grassroots groups in Kosovo that were beginning on their own to revive what she described as "civil society" in the province. This source suggested that there were, indeed, a variety of political views among Kosovar activists and that some of these activists appeared ready to engage in negotiation, but she cautioned that some activists take a more extreme position than the LDK. The recent publication by a dissident press in Belgrade of a collection of interviews with ten of the most prominent Kosovar political personalities confirms the diversity of positions among Kosovar leaders as well as the political sensitivity of perceived differences.[3]

The views expressed by Serbian journalists, academics, and activists in Belgrade clashed directly with official opinion. This was evident at the IMPP in the difference between Simic's views and those of the Foreign Ministry official. It was also made clear during our visit to the ministry, when we met with Deputy Foreign Minister Radoslav

Bulajic. Flanked by Pajic, as well as by his chief of staff and a coun-selor, Bulajic proceeded to present the official Serbian position in the most uncompromising terms. He asserted that the government was open to any kind of dialogue with the Kosovar Albanians. But, "because Kosovo is a strictly internal issue of Serbia and the FRY, no interna-tional mediation is necessary." Nor would the government, as his answers to several attempts to probe this position made clear, allow any third-party involvement in such dialogue.

The ministry officials asserted that the Kosovar Albanians reject the rights formally granted by the current (1990) Yugoslav constitu-tion and refuse to participate in negotiations for fear of compromising their pursuit of outright independence. This was an apparent reference to the fact that the Kosovars have boycotted elections in Yugoslavia, a strategy intended to underscore their refusal to legitimate the Yugoslav regime. "Separatism is their only goal," ministry officials argued. The chief of the American department, for example, argued that the 1981 unrest in Kosovo represented the refusal of Albanians to accept the extensive autonomy established under the 1974 con-stitution, and their "inability" to limit their aspirations and strategic goals. Thus, the official view throws full responsibility for the cur-rent deadlock onto the Kosovars. Moreover, these officials denied that there were any tensions in Kosovo, asserted that there was no vio-lence in the province, and attempted to assure the delegation that the government would do its best to implement the rights contained in the existing Serbian constitution.

Serbian President Milosevic conveyed essentially the same official perspective in his lengthy comments to the delegation on the situation in Kosovo, which he delivered in English. President Milosevic offered the delegation a well-known explanation for the Serbian attachment to Kosovo: "Kosovo is the heart of Serbia," he told us. "All our histo-ry is in Kosovo. For every Serb Kosovo is a holy thing." He attributed the widespread popular participation of Kosovo Albanians in the boy-cott of Serbian institutions to "terror" exercised against them by "nationalist extremists." He rationalized repression as a response to a separatist attempt in 1981 and ensuing Albanian nationalist activi-ties. He, too, denied the existence of current tensions in the province. He asserted that there is no conflict between Albanians and Serbs, only between Albanian separatists and the Serbian government: "We don't have any kind of conflict with Albanians in Kosovo. The prob-lem is the existence of a separatist movement or group of extremists with their aim as disintegration of Kosovo from Serbia and its merger with Albania." And, later: "We have never said 'Albanians' are the problem—only 'separatists.'"

Milosevic offered a startlingly different view of Kosovo from that which can be developed on the basis of numerous international sources and from the personal experiences of members of the delegation. He argued that charges that there is no freedom, that the region is subject to police repression, and that there is terror and fear "are not true at all." He argued that there are no restrictions on travel to the province, that ("in recent years") no one has been killed there "except our police," that there are no political prisoners, that Albanians are equal citizens, that newspapers are free to attack the government, and that there is no censorship.

Milosevic argued that Kosovo was an internal issue that "cannot be internationalized." He threw the onus for the present deadlock on "separatist extremists" and asserted that "we cannot please extremists and would be crazy to try." Yet, he did show an awareness that some kind of initiative was necessary to break this deadlock and that what was needed was "both internal and external initiatives." The delegation queried him about what kind of initiatives he might be preparing, and he informed us of proposals now under consideration to devolve increased authority to local (*opstina*, or county, level) institutions, and to establish local decisionmaking institutions based on interethnic consensus. He also intimated that alternative ethnic Albanian leaders "influential enough to get the masses to participate" might soon emerge to break the political monopoly now exercised by the LDK. It is not clear how such initiatives might contribute to a solution.

In the context of a discussion of U.S.-Serbia relations, the delegation suggested to Milosevic that a positive confidence-building measure and step toward solution of the Kosovo problem might be to allow the opening of a U.S. Information Agency (USIA) office in Prishtina, as the U.S. government had long requested. He agreed to this proposal. Following the meeting, the delegation informed U.S. officials of Milosevic's agreement and, upon returning to the United States, several members of the delegation met with Assistant Secretary of State Richard Holbrooke to emphasize the opportunity they thought this agreement represented. In early January Holbrooke announced that a USIA office would be established; the announcement was confirmed by Secretary of State Warren Christopher after his meeting with Milosevic in Belgrade in early February. The ability to reach agreement on this issue underscores Milosevic's interest in cooperation with the Unietd States, which derives from the fact that the United States has now assumed the leading role in the Balkans and holds the keys to lifting sanctions, to international recognition, to the solution of outstanding political issues in Bosnia-Herzegovina, and to other benefits that Milosevic seeks to achieve. This interest creates an opportunity to pursue further efforts of this kind in relation to the Kosovo question.

Milosevic's discussion of possible future changes in Kosovo also suggested that the Serbian leadership was considering redrawing *opstina* boundaries. This statement raised the question whether redrawing the boundaries might lead to a partition of Kosovo, as a prelude to granting independence to a truncated province. In a later conversation between the delegation and independent Belgrade journalists, one of the country's most acute political observers (a staunch critic of Milosevic) suggested spontaneously that partition—with Serbs taking about 20 percent of the province (Serbs now constitute less than 10 percent of the population)—represented an undesirable but realistic solution to the problem. He had come to this position, he said, because the Albanians of Kosovo were simply too deeply alienated and would not accept even a high level of autonomy. Re-integration was "inconceivable" to him; even more difficult to imagine than the re-integration of Bosnia. Partition, another journalist explained, would assign the Orthodox monastery towns of Gracanica, Decani, and Pec and the mining complex of Trepca to Serbia. It should be noted, however, that such a division would be economically favorable to the Serbs and thus difficult for Albanian leaders to accept. Moreover, such a partition might weaken Serbia's claim to retain other minority-populated territories. Partition would almost certainly destabilize Macedonia by encouraging secessionist tendencies among Albanians there.

Our visit to Belgrade left us with the impression that there might be some opportunity for discussions between Serbian and Kosovar leaders, if the talks could be structured properly. Although the time did not appear to be ripe for direct, official negotiations, nongovernmental organizations could play a valuable role by hosting unofficial, or "second-track," dialogues like those that led to the Oslo agreement between Israel and the PLO. Indeed, Micunovic's Democratic Center, working with the Project on Ethnic Relations (a nongovernmental organization based in Princeton, New Jersey, headed by American scholar Allen Kassof) and the Forum on InterEthnic Relations organized by Belgrade professor and democratic activist Dusan Janjic, had hosted such discussions in Belgrade in June 1995. Although these talks were marked by obvious differences between the Kosovar and Serbian participants, they also produced agreement on the need to continue contact and discussions.[4] The dramatically changed international circumstances in the wake of the Dayton agreement and the changes that these appear to have induced among some important Serbian actors now make it possible to build on the achievements of the Democratic Center and the Project on Ethnic Relations. To do so will require more flexibility on both sides than was shown in June. On the Serbian side, this means resolving the contradictions between pragmatic and dogmatic approaches in favor of the former. A similar change is required on the side of the Kosovars, as well.

PRISHTINA

The delegation traveled directly from Belgrade to Prishtina, where it met with members of the LDK executive committee, including Fehmi Agani, Hydajet Hyseni, Rexhep Ismajli, and Naip Zeka. The attitudes and positions expressed by members of the LDK executive committee at first seemed to leave relatively little room for optimism about such change.

Agani's straightforward presentation of the official LDK position stressed that the goal of the LDK was independence, not autonomy. A brief summary of the repression that has taken place in Kosovo was followed by the argument that, because Yugoslavia no longer exists, and because Albanian membership in Yugoslavia was the expression of the Albanians' right to self-determination, they now were entitled to express that right once again (that is, to establish their own independent state). This interpretation of the conditions under which Kosovo became a part of Yugoslavia ignored its status as a part of Serbia since the Treaty of Bucharest of 1913. The territory that is now Kosovo was ceded to Serbia following the defeat of the Ottoman Empire in the first Balkan War. The border established in 1913 between Albania on one side and Serbia and Macedonia on the other has not changed since (except for the Italian occupation during World War II). The LDK leaders asserted that Kosovo had been the equal of the federal republics under the 1974 constitution and therefore had the same right to declare its independence as the former republics that now enjoy international recognition. This claim exaggerated Kosovo's constitutional status under the old Yugoslav regime and, therefore, its "right" to independence. But it reflected the political reality of the regime as it functioned in the period 1972–81: Kosovo enjoyed extensive autonomy across a broad range of areas. After the adoption of the 1974 constitution, it enjoyed de facto equal, although de jure inferior, status in federal decisionmaking. In practice, however, it remained subordinated to the Serbian republic both constitutionally and in such key areas as security affairs.[5] Thus, especially in light of developments since 1991, the political and constitutional history of the province and its relationship to Serbia presents a mixed picture.

Although interpretation of the 1974 Yugoslav constitution was touched upon in several ensuing discussions in Macedonia and Albania, for the LDK executive committee members such debates were essentially irrelevant. They insisted quite simply that Yugoslavia had ceased to exist and that the present FRY is an illegitimate state. The FRY was established, in their view, by illegal means, with Kosovo included against the will of the Kosovar Albanians. They assert an unrestricted claim to sovereignty over the territory of the province.[6]

The LDK executive committee members displayed somewhat conflicting attitudes toward gradualism and compromise. They clearly wanted to appear willing to compromise in principle. But in this discussion they were unwilling to budge an inch on the essentials of their position—that is, independence. They expressed support for establishing an international presence in Kosovo as a step toward negotiations. But they argued that such presence had not prevented repression in the past, so that any future presence would have to be accompanied by "demilitarization of the region and establishment of a civil administration." It seems clear that by "civil" they mean local Albanian administration.

They were careful to specify that movement toward a solution could not take the form of steps that would recognize Kosovo as part of Serbia. "We know that there will be gradual movement. But we think that gradualism should not begin with an act that confirms that Kosova is an internal issue of Serbia." Resistance to recognition of being part of Serbia extends even to the idea of a democratic Serbia. As one Kosovar put it, "A democratic Serbia would recognize the right of Albanians to self-determination. The test of such a Serbia would be its attitude toward Albanian self-determination."

The LDK has become a deeply entrenched nationalist leadership. Its president, Ibrahim Rugova, enjoys substantial international prestige as a result of his having organized and maintained a peaceful movement for independence, refusing to turn to violence. Members of the LDK leadership reported that the party has established an international network of supporters and is able to raise significant financial resources from ethnic Albanian emigre communities. Inside Kosovo, it has created a network of parallel institutions that reinforce the Albanian population's boycott of official institutions, which are seen as expressions of Serbian occupation. Serbian authorities do not permit the alternative parliament to function. Elected in 1992 at the same time that Rugova was elected president of the alternative, or parallel state ("Republic of Kosova"), members of the alternative parliament have been subjected to Serbian repression, and many have fled the country.

The alternative school system does operate, however, which allows the population to boycott the official school system, from whose curriculum Albanian culture was completely eliminated by the Serbian government. The LDK also sponsors an alternative university in an attempt to mitigate the effect of Serbia's having eliminated Albanian-language instruction from the University of Prishtina. Education thus serves as an important instrument for maintaining popular support for the LDK leadership and reinforcing nationalism.

The elimination of the Albanian curriculum from the official school system and the resort to a parallel system undermines the quality of education being delivered to a whole generation of Kosovars. At the invitation of the LDK, members of the delegation visited some alternative schools. The secondary school operated under extremely trying conditions. It was badly overcrowded (850 students using twelve classrooms in three shifts). Students were packed shoulder to shoulder in both the ancient history and the mathematics classes we visited. Overcrowding was made more serious by dangerous physical conditions. The school operated in an unfinished three-story private home (on loan to the LDK for this purpose by its owner). There were no railings on the crowded central stairway and a distinct lack of heat in the classrooms. (Students were bundled up even on what was a not very cold day.) There was an obvious lack of textbooks and other materials, a lack that was compounded by problems in staffing. Most instructors are former teachers in the state system, but new teachers are now being hired from among the graduates of the parallel university. The lower level of preparation of these teachers will accelerate the decline in quality of the alternative system as a whole. The severe problems of quality may be one reason why, for some of even the most committed nationalists among the Kosovars, restoring the local public school system to normal operation is a very high priority and represents an incentive to compromise.

Cultural figures associated with the LDK are engaged in ongoing efforts to "nationalize" the curriculum of the alternative school system. As one prominent Kosovar intellectual explained, "We have our own curriculum, and it has nothing to do with Belgrade and the Serbian curriculum. It resists involvement with Serbia." He went on to argue that "ideology has been wiped out from our curriculum, and the heritage that has been banned for fifty years has been recovered." Even though pressed directly on this issue, he would not or could not recognize that the effort to create a nationalist curriculum was simply the substitution of one ideology for another, rather than its elimination. With respect to "subjects of national [in the cultural sense] importance," he reported that a common curriculum was being developed with Albania for elementary and secondary schools. A joint committee has been established for linguistics, literature, national history, the arts, and music.

The adamant views articulated by Albanian activists in our formal meetings contrasted with the desire for "normalization" expressed privately by one Kosovar attending the LDK dinner. "Normalization" in this context can be defined as full restoration of the human rights of Kosovars and of the political rights enjoyed by Kosovo under the provisions of the 1974 constitution. For some Kosovars, including this participant, normalization of the educational system appears to have assumed central importance and would represent a major step forward. The delegation had limited opportunity to explore opinions other than those within the leadership of the LDK. A meeting with local government officials represented nothing more than a repeat performance of the official positions we heard from the Yugoslav Foreign Ministry and the Serbian president in Belgrade.

The delegation did not have the opportunity to familiarize itself with independent grassroots activity taking place in Kosovo outside the control of either the Serb authorities or the LDK. Others with first-hand knowledge of Kosovo report that various groups have organized themselves autonomously to pursue local social, political, and cultural improvements, as well as private economic opportunities. These sources caution that a greater range of views can be found among Kosovar Albanians when one has time to develop broader and deeper contact with the population. Some Kosovar Albanians, including some prominent political figures, are said to be willing to explore privately the possibility of compromise with Serbia.

This perspective—that more is possible than might at first seem evident—is consistent with what the delegation learned during a private dinner with another leading Kosovar political figure. He raised the possibility that even the LDK leadership might show some flexibility and that some form of compromise with Serbia might be found that would establish a short-term modus vivendi and permit lengthier negotiations over a long-term solution. He acknowledged that relations between the LDK and Serbia had reached a dead end. He suggested that, if left to itself, such a situation would lead to war. But he also suggested that the LDK was ready to negotiate and to be "flexible." He described a possible interim solution as the establishment of "1974 plus"—meaning restoration of the autonomy enjoyed by Kosovo under the 1974 Yugoslav constitution, but with the additional recognition that Yugoslavia no longer existed. This proposal would require negotiations over the future status of the region that might last five years. This approach did not mean, he emphasized, that the Kosovars were forgoing their claim to independence. Rather, it meant that they "accept independence of Kosova as a process," and that that process would involve long and detailed negotiation with Serbia.

The parallels between this position and that articulated by some Serbs during our discussions in Belgrade suggest an opportunity to foster meaningful dialogue between the two sides. But clearer and more authoritative support for such a dialogue than the delegation was able to secure would have to be obtained from both sides for such dialogue, let alone a significant agreement, to take place. In a follow-up visit to Belgrade in mid-February 1996, Steven L. Burg, consultant to the working group, found that our Serbian interlocutors were unwilling or unable to secure such support. The reshuffling of personnel at the congress of the ruling Socialist Party of Serbia in early March and the crackdown on the independent media and the Soros Foundation in Yugoslavia introduced new uncertainties into the task of securing clear support for such a dialogue. Two prominent Kosovar intellectuals, in separate discussions, each expressed support for the idea of implementing an interim agreement while negotiations over a more lasting solution continued. But each also observed that such discussions would have to receive the mandate of President Rugova to be considered legitimate. And the Serbian participants would have to have a similar mandate from the Serbian leadership. In the words of one of these Kosovar intellectuals, "there is not much use in discussion by people from the margins of society."

MACEDONIA

The delegation traveled from Prishtina to Skopje, where, after a briefing from the U.S. Liaison Office, it began immediately to explore the sources of tensions in relations between the ethnic Albanians and Macedonians in Macedonia. The problem in Macedonia differs in important ways from that in Kosovo. Politics in Macedonia is far more open and pluralistic than in Kosovo. As described above, several political parties compete for support in the ethnic Albanian community in Macedonia, and two Albanian parties have won seats in parliament (as have Albanians who are independent or members of nonethnic parties). One Albanian party participates in the government coalition.

The delegation familiarized itself with the positions now being articulated in the Albanian community through a series of meetings with party leaders and activists. The largest ethnic Albanian party, as previously described, is the PPD. It holds ten seats in the parliament elected in 1994 and presently governs both Tetovo (in coalition with the Macedonian nationalist party known as VMRO-DPMNE, in its Macedonian acronym) and Gostivar. The delegation met with three representatives of the PPD in the Tetovo party headquarters. Ilir Luma, a member of the party's presidium, complained about the "marginalization" of Albanians in Macedonia, claiming that they are second-class citizens. More specifically, Abdylmenat Bexheti, an economist, reported that Albanians had been excluded from decisionmaking about, and participation in, the transformation and privatization of the economy. He attributed this to the prior exclusion of Albanians from the Communist elite and the current monopoly over privatization exercised by that elite. He also claimed that Albanians constituted only about 4 percent of employees in the public sector, including those in the Ministry of Internal Affairs (police). When pressed for recommendations to rectify these problems and for specific elements of their party program, however, the representatives of the PPD mentioned only the need to support the Albanian-language university established in Tetovo the previous year.

The delegation next met with the secretary of the People's Democratic Party (*Partia Demokratike Popullore*), also in Tetovo. This party has four seats in parliament compared to the PPD's ten seats. Iljaz Halimi outlined his party's differences with the PPD in the following way: He asserted that his party was working for the realization of the collective rights of Albanians, including the right of self-determination, because individual rights are derived from collective ones. He argued that Kosovo should be allowed to become its own state and that Albanians in Macedonia should be recognized as a constituent nation of Macedonia. This does not mean, he explained, that they would establish an independent state. But it does mean that Albanians would secure proportional representation and participation in local and state governing institutions, recognition of both Macedonian and Albanian as official languages, and Albanian-language education at all levels; in short, all the rights that Macedonians enjoy.

On the question of territorial autonomy, Halimi argued that the 1992 (unofficial) referendum organized by his party in Albanian-populated regions of the country, in which the ethnic Albanian population voted overwhelmingly in favor of territorial autonomy for the Albanian community in Macedonia, "expressed the will of the people" in light of the failure of the Macedonian leadership specifically to include the Albanians in their definition of the state. If the Macedonian government continues to ignore the demands of the Albanians, he stated, the People's Democratic Party will call for territorial autonomy within Macedonia. The demands that must be addressed include revision of the constitution and revision of the laws on citizenship, language use, self-government, and higher education. He also singled out the university in Tetovo as an issue that must be addressed by the government. Halimi legitimated his positions by repeated references to "pressure from our constituency to leave parliament" and to the fact that his party would be seen as "illegitimate" if it continued to participate while the government ignored Albanian demands.

Menduh Thaçi, leader of the radical breakaway faction of the PPD now known as the PPD-Sh, criticized both the government and the Albanian parties that participate in it. He characterized the Macedonian constitution as an "essentially anti-Albanian framework." He charged that the PPD entered the government simply to seek power. He singled out for particular criticism inequalities in population among electoral districts. Predominantly Macedonian districts had smaller populations than predominantly Albanian districts. He called for negotiations between the Albanian community and the Macedonian government with the participation of a third-party negotiator to draft a new constitution and establish a new common state.

The new state order that Thaçi had in mind would consist of a bicameral legislature with a "house of nationalities" in which decisionmaking would be based on "consensus." (Such institutions would resemble those in the former Yugoslavia.) The Albanian and Macedonian languages would be equal and have official status throughout the country, including in the educational system. He identified the establishment of "proportionality in representation and participation in government" as "the critical issue." He went on to elaborate somewhat differently on these points:

> The satisfaction of our demands can be achieved only with the participation of a third party, because we have no trust in the government. The government is excommunist. Its

Western orientation is not sincere. In five to seven years, when Russia and Serbia return to the scene as powers, Macedonia will reform its anticommunism in that direction. This can be prevented only brutally, only if Albanians can gain a veto in Macedonia of the kind that only the West can give them.

When asked by the delegation why he trusted the West, Thaçi responded, "because this is a question of an Orthodox/Slavic axis and an Islamic fundamentalist axis, neither of which the Albanians belong to." To support this vision of an emergent Orthodox Slavic/Islamic Fundamentalist alliance and its hostility to the Albanians, Thaçi claimed that members of the government had recently been happy to attend the opening of an Islamic theological faculty but remained adamantly opposed to the university in Tetovo.

The most conflictual issues at present are those surrounding higher education, including language use and the status of the university in Tetovo. The delegation's first meeting was with Emilija Simoska, then the minister of education, who outlined the government's attempts to accommodate Albanian demands for Albanian-language instruction at the university level.[7] She pointed out that new laws allow the pedagogical faculties to use minority languages for the entire curriculum and that groups of subjects elsewhere in the university would be offered in minority languages as long as the use of the language related to an effort to "preserve the culture."[8] The minister called this policy, adopted by government decree, "an interpretation in the spirit of the constitution." This is an apparent reference to article 48 of the Macedonian constitution, which guarantees minorities the right "freely to express, foster and develop their identity and national attributes," as well as the right to establish "scholarly and other associations" through which to do so. Thus, she pointed to instruction in Turkish and Albanian in existing university-level theater programs as examples of the kind of activity made possible by this policy. This approach, however, remains subject to review by the constitutional court as the result of a legal challenge brought against government policies. The court still may declare these policies unconstitutional.

The proposed law on higher education stipulates in article 9 that higher educational activity is to be carried out in Macedonian.[9] Classes may be conducted in the languages of the nationalities in departments of elementary and secondary educational pedagogy, at teachers colleges, and in certain other subjects in order to preserve and develop cultural and national identity. These provisions would establish a legal basis for the policy described by the minister and are seen as concessions by the government. Albanian leaders, however, regard the law as highly restric-tive, a measure that fails to address their demands for more compre-hensive higher educational opportunities in the Albanian language. It is not surprising, therefore, that the minister reported that "90 percent of the [parliamentary] debate in the first round was about article 9."

The education minister also pointed to "affirmative action" efforts to increase the enrollment of ethnic Albanian students in the state-financed university in Skopje (and its campus in Bitola) as evi-dence of the government's good-faith efforts to meet the demands of Albanians for greater opportunities for higher education. She report-ed that the government has established a quota of 10 percent, over and above established enrollment levels, for the enrollment of ethnic Albanians at Skopje University. She argued that part of the difficul-ty of enrolling Albanian students was due to the poor quality of instruction in Albanian-language secondary schools and the fact that the entrance exam for Skopje University was given only in Macedonian. Nonetheless, according to the minister, enrollment of Albanians had increased from 1.3 to 9.7 percent of the student body over the past three years. These figures differed from those cited later by the prime minister, who reported that "not even 3 percent of the 10 percent" set-aside had been filled over the past two years. One of the ethnic Albanian party leaders with whom the delegation met alleged that Albanian enrollment was substantially lower. Despite these discrepancies, it seems clear that the government is committed to a strategy of "affirmative action" to increase Albanian enrollment in the university, even if it has failed to implement it successfully up to now.

Macedonian nationalist opposition also constrains the govern-ment from responding to Albanian demands. The VMRO-DPMNE (commonly referred to as VMRO) is the most outspokenly nationalist Macedonian party. The Democratic Party and the Movement for Pan-Macedonian Action also oppose the governing coalition from Macedonian nationalist positions. During our meeting with leaders of VMRO, the delegation heard attacks on the government for signing the September 1995 interim accord normalizing relations with Greece, assertions that most Macedonians do not support the treaty, accusa-tions that the government gerrymandered voting districts to reduce the electoral strength of its opponents, charges that the government falsi-fied the 1994 election results, and outright rejection of "the extreme demands of the Albanian parties." The VMRO representatives opposed the use of Albanian in higher educational institutions as well as the affirmative action policies of the government. They did assert, however, that they were in favor of upholding the minority rights of all groups "in accordance with international norms."

The VMRO enjoys its strongest support among Macedonians in the heavily Albanian-populated western districts of the country. This support reflects the deep split between the Albanian and Macedonian communities in these areas. In the 1990 elections support for VMRO increased dramatically in the second round of voting as the result of a backlash among Macedonian voters reacting to the strength shown by ethnic Albanian parties in the first round. As a result, VMRO was the numerically largest party in the first postcommunist parliament. It could not, however, form a majority coalition. In the October 1994 elections VMRO reacted to the strong first-round showing by the Social Democratic Alliance of Macedonia and its coalition partners by calling for a boycott of the second round of voting. This resulted in a sharp decline in turnout (from 78 to less than 58 percent), but it also resulted in the exclusion of VMRO from parliament.

In ethnically mixed regions of western Macedonia, each community votes for its own nationalist party. This has produced an unusual power-sharing arrangement in Tetovo, where the population is almost 75 percent Albanian. Here, the ethnically Albanian PPD and the Macedonian nationalist VMRO share governmental power. This uneasy coalition was forged largely as a result of their common opposition to the local communists. According to Tetovo officials, the last Communist government refused to give up power for a year until the PPD and VMRO united against it. The tension between the Macedonian and Albanian communities in Gostivar was more difficult to overcome. There the local government is run entirely by members of the PPD, which won forty of the fifty seats in the local council. The local Macedonians refused to share power with the PPD. They organized a boycott of the local council and of the seats reserved for them in the local government and blockaded local government headquarters for a year and a half. They were still refusing to participate when the working group visited Gostivar in December 1995.

A similarly uncompromising attitude toward the demands of the Albanian minority was displayed by the leader of a more moderate opposition party, the Democratic Party. In a separate meeting, he argued that Albanian demands would inevitably lead to the disintegration of Macedonia. To base rights on ethnic identity, he argued, would lead to the "Bosnification" or "Yugoslavization" of Macedonia and directly to war. He proposed instead an avowedly liberal notion of the state as a state of "equal citizens" without regard for ethnic identity. He warned, however, that extremist views were becoming more powerful in the Albanian community. One source of the problem for Macedonia, he pointed out, was the persistence of the Kosovo problem. Extremism in Macedonia was, in his view, an "imported ideology" brought by Albanians from Kosovo. Thus, resolution of the Kosovo problem would alleviate the ethnic conflict in Macedonia. But the solution of Kosovo, he warned, had to be achieved within the framework of Yugoslavia (that is, without secession of Kosovo) in order not to destabilize Macedonia.

Resistance among ethnic Macedonians to sharing power, resources, and opportunities with ethnic Albanians may be attributed to a certain degree of simple prejudice toward the Albanians. But it is also rooted in the fears Macedonians feel about the prospects for their own survival as a nation. To concede to Albanian demands might weaken their control over the state's institutional defenses against perceived threats to Macedonian identity from Bulgaria and Greece, as well as Albania, not to mention Serbia. Yet, this resistance to accommodation appears to be making matters worse.

HIGHER EDUCATION

The reestablishment of Albanian-language instruction at the pedagogical faculty in Skopje (abolished as part of the post-1981 Yugoslavian crackdown on Albanian culture), for example, came only after a long dispute over this issue that pitted the government against recalcitrant elements in the university unwilling to make concessions to the Albanian minority. In explaining why it took so long for the government to satisfy demands for Albanian-language instruction at the university level, prime minister of Macedonia Branko Crvenkovski described to the delegation the university's efforts to use professional criteria and standards of quality to resist "political interference" in academic questions such as admissions and enrollment. He pointed out that, eventually, the government prevailed. But in the case of the pedagogical faculty, which was the original focus of Albanian demands, the struggle between university and government lasted three years.

The prime minister's account of this struggle was corroborated during the delegation's meeting with a faculty member from the university, who reported that the rector of Skopje University resisted pressures for change from both the minister of education and the faculty. The delegation listened in dismay to this professor's account of how a department (faculty) that wanted to undermine the appeal of the university in Tetovo by admitting to Skopje University more Albanian students from an unexpectedly large applicant pool was stymied by the rector's refusal to allow expanded enrollment. The faculty member noted, however, that even before the present escalation of tensions most ethnic Albanian students went to study in Prishtina "because they felt more comfortable there" and because "students who failed entrance exams for Skopje University could still enroll in the University of Prishtina." Thus, it is not discrimination alone that depresses Albanian enrollment in Skopje; it is also the inadequate preparation of Albanian secondary school graduates and the greater attraction of attending a culturally Albanian institution. A policy of "affirmative action" in university admissions cannot change these factors by itself.

The changes that are taking place now may represent "too little, too late" to satisfy the more radical elements in the Albanian community. For this reason, one of the independent journalists with whom the delegation met in Skopje characterized the delay in responding to Albanian demands for higher education as "a *big* mistake." While the dispute over Albanian-language instruction in Skopje University unfolded, Albanian nationalists organized a university of their own in Tetovo. Two ethnic Albanian members of parliament affiliated with the Liberal Party, which was then a member of the governing coalition and which "accepts Macedonia as a homeland—as *our* homeland," had a similar view of this delay. Xhemil Idrizi and Isa Ramadani argued that it was the failure to establish an Albanian-language pedagogical faculty in Skopje that created the conditions leading to establishment of the university in Tetovo.

The issue of the university in Tetovo is seen very differently by ethnic Albanian and Macedonian leaders. Ethnic Albanians define the effort to establish an Albanian university in Macedonia as an attempt to meet the educational needs of the ethnic Albanian population of the country. Macedonian leaders view the effort as a self-consciously political step toward establishing parallel Albanian institutions in Macedonia akin to those in Kosovo. It is not surprising, therefore, that the opening of the university in Tetovo in February 1995 was the occasion of a violent confrontation between the government and Albanian demonstrators, resulting in many injuries and one death. That incident represented a culmination of growing intergroup tensions in the country. Several of those with whom the delegation met—Albanian and

Macedonian—observed that the shock of that event contributed to a marked reduction in tensions, as both ethnic Albanian leaders and the government appear to have been chastened by the prospect of violence. These tensions, however, appeared to be on the rise again. The exclusion of "the Albanian question" from the Dayton accords angered and disappointed Albanian activists all across the region, while the accords' recognition of Serbian and Muslim-Croat "entities" within Bosnia also increased expectations that partition and a redrawing of borders may now be possible.

The delegation found uniform support for the university in Tetovo across the entire spectrum of Albanian leaders and activists with whom it met. Sometimes this support was offered spontaneously, without any prompting from the delegation. Local government officials in Gostivar, for example, immediately singled out the university in Tetovo when asked what was the most important issue facing the Albanian community— this, despite the long litany of their complaints about the inadequacies of local authority and resources to meet the needs of their constituents. The university in Tetovo appears to have taken on transcendent importance for the Albanians in Macedonia.

Part of the widespread support for the university can be interpreted as a reaction to the failure of the government, and especially the Social Democratic Alliance of Macedonia (SDSM, in its Macedonian acronym), which dominates the government coalition, to act on the issue. PPD, also a member of the coalition, explained to the delegation in Tetovo that SDSM had accepted a PPD demand that the government address the question of Albanian education (as well as "increase the number of Albanians employed in government, [and] respect the elementary national rights of the Albanians to use their mother tongue and national symbols"), but "nothing has happened." The university in Tetovo, they explained, was founded in response to the increased need for Albanian-language instruction in the wake of the closure of the University of Prishtina by Serbia and the failure of the Macedonian government to address this need. The rector of the university in Tetovo, Fadil Suleimani, also acknowledged that the closing of the University of Prishtina and the economic and political exclusion of ethnic Albanians from other regions of the former Yugoslavia had contributed to the demand for an Albanian-language institution of higher education in Macedonia. But he emphasized that the founding of the university in Tetovo was an educational, not a political action. This view was shared by several of our Albanian interlocutors. Suleimani summarized his view of the university by suggesting that it was "an existential need" of the Albanian community.

Ethnically Macedonian government officials insist that the motive for founding the university in Tetovo was political, not educational, and they seem unwilling to compromise. According to Prime Minister Branko Crvenkovski, "The entire initiative is not an educational one, but a political one," which he attributed to activists from Kosovo. This view appears "true" in the sense that many of the Albanian activists we met and who are involved in the issue spent many years in Kosovo, even though some were born in Macedonia. There is a clear fear among Macedonians that the establishment of an Albanian university is a step toward setting up the kind of parallel institutions that have been established in Kosovo. Indeed, the prime minister argued, "We are ready to support all initiatives to support national rights of minorities that do not lead to disintegration and parallel institutions." He warned explicitly that "no initiative should create parallel institutions." Such fears of separatism are undoubtedly reinforced by the pronounced tendency of Albanian political figures to speak in terms of a single, united Albanian nation, of which the Albanians of Macedonia are only a part. This was characteristic even of the leaders of the moderate PPD.

The interpretation of the university in Tetovo offered by the director of intelligence and counterintelligence of the Ministry of Interior, Dobri Velickovski, was also quite unsympathetic, but rather different. He argued that Suleimani, the driving force behind the establishment of the university in Tetovo, "had been sent by the Serbs from Prishtina, where he was *not* being harassed, to create a provocation. From a police perspective, this was a distinct attempt on the part of Serbia to create unrest in order to provide a pretext for intervention." This interpretation was, according to the head of the Soros Foundation of Macedonia, the subject of rumors in Macedonia but was then replaced by another—false—rumor that the American financier and philanthropist George Soros was behind the university. Velickovski alleged that the university is supported by Albania, which sends professors to lecture at the university "without any registration or permission, and even gives them diplomatic passports." Despite the delegation's many conversations about the university in Tetovo with Albanians and Macedonians, we did not hear this from another source. The interpretation offered by the intelligence official, however, reflects the widely held perception that events in Kosovo and developments in Macedonia are linked, as well as the continuing high levels of mutual distrust characteristic of intergroup relations in the region.

The only ethnically Macedonian political figure who offered a conciliatory approach to this issue was Vasil Tupurkovski, formerly a rising younger member of the Macedonian Communist elite in Yugoslavia and the last Macedonian member of the state presidency under the old order. He urged that the government allow the university to exist as a private institution, neither recognizing, financing, nor banning it. At the same time, he stressed the need to expand opportunities for Albanians to study at Skopje University. He, too, viewed the university in Tetovo as a politically motivated phenomenon, but he argued that the best strategy for dealing with the nationalist challenge it represented is to give moderate Albanian leaders a chance to deliver real benefits to their constituencies in order to turn popular support away from the radicals. He argued that technical tasks such as providing secure water to localities provided an opportunity for the government to strengthen the legitimacy of moderate local leaders. Once moderates were "meeting the real needs of the population, they might then address larger principles without being considered automatically anti-Albanian." This perspective is consistent with that offered by moderate Albanians. Parliament members Idrizi and Ramadani, for example, argued that even within the context of the new law on higher education it might be possible to define Tetovo as a private institution and thereby legalize the use of Albanian as the language of instruction. These views suggest that a conciliatory approach to the issue of the university in Tetovo might help strengthen moderates on both sides.

GOVERNMENT AND POLITICS

The Albanian university in Tetovo is not, however, the only issue over which the Albanian minority and the government are struggling. Local government officials in Tetovo and Gostivar, regardless of ethnicity, decry the extensive control over local affairs exercised by Skopje. The administration of public affairs remains a highly centralized system, with a large role played by local prefects appointed directly by the central government in Skopje. The delegation heard complaints that local governments do not control enough resources (for example, tax receipts) or command enough administrative or legislative authority to address the real needs of their populations. Local officials viewed the new law on local government as inadequate in this respect as well.

From the perspective of local ethnic Albanian populations, the extensive central control still characteristic of the Macedonian state also has cultural and ethnic dimensions. The constitution provides for use of minority languages only by local governments, not by local offices of the central government. As one ethnic Albanian official in Tetovo

explained it, since the central government exercises so much authority over public affairs, and because all offices of the central government
must conduct their business in Macedonian, ethnic Albanian citizens in
largely Albanian areas find they cannot carry out their interactions
with government in their own language. This official suggested that
language use should be determined at the local level. He pointed out
that Albanians enjoyed more rights with respect to language use under
the 1974 Yugoslav constitution than they do now. The intergroup tension just below the surface in Tetovo was indicated when an official
representing the ethnic Macedonian nationalist party VMRO coun-
tered that the central government should determine language use "so
that we don't have to do it."

Local leaders in Gostivar suggested that the central government
might be convinced to transfer more power to local governments if the
heavily Albanian-populated districts in the west were represented in
parliament in true proportion to their population. Local government
officials in both Tetovo and Gostivar echoed complaints made by several Albanian party leaders and activists about the deficiencies of electoral districting. The number of MPs elected from Tetovo, they charged,
was the same as the number elected from mainly Macedonian regions
with significantly smaller populations. This results in the underrepre-
sentation of ethnic Albanians in the parliament.

Given the strong pattern of ethnic voting in Macedonia, reducing
the number of positions open to competition within the Albanian-populated *opstinas* in the west reduces the chances for multiple political
perspectives to emerge within the Albanian community, or even for
cross-ethnic alliances to emerge. That political pluralism remains a possibility was suggested by the observations of Vladimir Milcin, the head
of the Soros Foundation of Macedonia, who noted the strong traditions of intergroup tolerance, living together, and respect for differences among the ethnically mixed urban populations of such western
cities as Debar. Simple electoral reforms may thus offer an opportunity
to encourage political pluralism in western Macedonia (and elsewhere)
and reduce the power of radical nationalists among Albanians there.

At present, the government is considering an electoral reform that
would make electoral districts more equal in population. The number of
seats in parliament would be increased to 140, with 20 of these allocated proportionally on the basis of countrywide vote totals. Several of the
Albanian political leaders with whom the delegation met had pressed for
the introduction of nationwide proportional representation. MPs Idrizi
and Ramadani conceded that the PPD and the more nationalist PPD-Sh

together commanded two-thirds of the Albanian electorate. But they argued that increasing the number of seats and introducing proportionality would allow the emergence of nonnationalist forces and the development of what they called civil society. They pointed out that, even under the existing majoritarian system, "the nationalist Albanian politicians expected to win everything [in the Albanian constituencies] but didn't." Idrizi and Ramadani preferred to see half the seats in parliament allocated proportionally. The actual impact of a proportional system would depend heavily on the precise electoral rules that are eventually adopted. These vary greatly among existing proportional systems.

Several Albanian party leaders and activists complained to the delegation about the exclusion of ethnic Albanians from employment in state institutions. The (ethnically Macedonian) head of the Soros Foundation made the more general argument that interethnic tensions might be reduced if the government moved quickly to increase opportunities for Albanians to participate in society. The delegation discussed personnel policy with several senior officials of the Macedonian government, including Stojan Andov, who was then acting president. "It is in the political interest of all Macedonians for Albanians to be fully represented and to participate fully in public life in Macedonia," Andov declared. He went on to assert that the government has "created a plan for opening the military and state administrations to Albanians: from the police to customs, to banks." But he cautioned the delegation that the ability of the government to impose personnel policy was limited: "What is private is private," he argued.

In a later meeting the defense minister, Blagoj Handziski, described the efforts of his ministry to increase the participation of Albanians. He reported that Albanians constitute approximately 16–22 percent of civilian employees of the ministry, a figure not much below their proportion in the population as recorded in the 1994 census. Albanians constitute a similar proportion of military recruits. Among professional soldiers, the proportion of Albanians increased from 0.1 percent overall in 1992 to 5.2 percent among noncommissioned officers and 3.0 percent among officers in 1995. In the military academy Albanian cadets increased from 2 to 12 percent of the first-year class. The language of command remains Macedonian with no apparent plans to introduce Albanian. In fact, the minister suggested that, because of Macedonia's interest in joining NATO, English would have to become the second language of command in the military. The minister reported, however, that "everyday military menus respect religious restrictions"—a reference to the Islamic prohibition on pork.

Director of Intelligence Velickovski also discussed the role of Albanians and other minorities in the Ministry of Internal Affairs. He pointed out that there has been an ethnic Albanian deputy minister since the mid-1960s, that Albanians are directors of several regional offices of the ministry, and that Albanians constitute 20–30 percent of all employees. Thus, at least in the military-security sector, it appears that the government is making a genuine effort to increase Albanian participation. It seems, however, that participation is expected to take place in the Macedonian language.

The government's mixed efforts to accommodate Albanian demands have placed its ethnic-Albanian coalition partner in a sensitive position. Members of the PPD confront the classic dilemma of the moderate ethnic party attempting to cooperate with a dominant majority in the face of intergroup tension: such cooperation is easily characterized as collaboration by more radical elements in the community. Members of parliament from the PPD thus did not vote for what their own government intended as conciliatory legislation on education. The dilemma faced by the government's Albanian coalition partners was recognized explicitly by the minister of education, who assured the delegation that although the PPD failed to support the new law on education in parliament, the draft had been "fully coordinated" beforehand among the government parties, including the PPD.

When members of the delegation asked PPD leaders why, in light of their differences with the SDSM, they remained in government, they acknowledged that "the dilemma is to continue to be part of government or find another forum." They suggested, however, that "if we choose to leave the government, it would be more difficult for all . . . and dangerous and hard for the region." They noted that "already we have popular reactions of dissatisfaction with participation in government. [We have] opponents among the Albanians themselves who want to establish parallel institutions here, and therefore we can have dangerous positions here." Their obvious concern about being outflanked politically by more extreme nationalists was clearly shared by each of the Albanian party leaders with whom we met, except for Thaçi of the PPD-Sh, who represents that extreme.

Shortly after the delegation returned from the Balkans, the prospect that the Albanian parties, including the government's coalition partner, might withdraw from parliament entirely was raised once again. PPD president Abdurahman Aliti, for example, suggested in an interview in *Nova Makedonija* in late December that the government's stand on higher education indicated a lack of goodwill and that the party might therefore choose to end its cooperation. A more general walkout of Albanian members of parliament was suggested in a media report originating in Albania at about the same time. Such a development would move Macedonian-Albanian ethnic relations closer to the deadlock characteristic of Kosovo.

Deadlock is something the Macedonian leadership cannot afford. Any threat by the Albanians to secede would immediately call into question the survival of the rest of the republic in the face of possible Serbian, Bulgarian, and Greek territorial pretensions. In the cabinet reshuffle carried out in February, the Liberal Party was expelled from the governing coalition for not having supported the government in parliament. But the PPD received five of seventeen ministerial posts, one more than in the previous government.[10] Thus, a coalition between moderates on both sides of the ethnic cleavage appears to have been preserved. It remains to be seen, however, whether the SDSM-PPD coalition is based on substantive policy agreement on any of the controversies that have contributed to ethnic tensions in the republic.

Macedonia may be facing increasingly difficult economic conditions. Former Macedonian member of the Yugoslav presidency Vasil Tupurkovski reported, for example, that Macedonia had benefited from sanctions against Serbia, because Serb entrepreneurs seeking to circumvent sanctions had shifted operations to Macedonia. The result was an influx of business to Macedonia. That business began to shift back to Serbia immediately with the lifting of sanctions. This loss of business, he claimed, was already depressing the Macedonian economy. The arms embargo imposed as a result of the post-Yugoslav wars prevented expansion of the military sector in the first years of Macedonian independence. As a result, a greater share of existing resources could be devoted to social development. With the end of the embargo, however, and the government's interest in gaining admission to NATO, resources will likely be drained away from social investment. That may place additional strains on relations between groups. As the prime minister suggested when he noted the negative short-term consequences of privatization, "All problems seem bigger on an empty stomach." The prospect of increased economic hardship only increases the incentive to solve the political problems between ethnic Albanians and Macedonians more quickly.

Prime Minister Crvenkovski made it very clear during his lengthy meeting with the delegation that he welcomed international efforts to reduce interethnic conflict in Macedonia. He suggested that such an effort might begin in Kosovo given that region's impact on events in

Macedonia. Yet, he also warned against attempting a multilateral regional approach to the Albanian issue because it might lead to "an 'integral' solution"; that is, the attempt to forge a "greater Albania." "It is very important," he argued, "for Albanians in Macedonia to make the decision about Albanians in Macedonia, not Tirana or Prishtina." Similarly, he argued, the Kosovo question had to be resolved in the framework of the FRY. The reasoning behind this position is clear: the Macedonian leadership is resistant to any action it perceives as dividing Macedonia, administratively or culturally. The tenor of our meetings with Macedonian Albanians suggests that any partition of Kosovo from the FRY could lead to efforts to partition Macedonia. Finally, the prime minister cautioned the delegation to remember that "the source of conflict is not always among the minority. It can come from the majority." He underscored the constraining effect on the government of ethnic Macedonian nationalism and extremism.

TIRANA

The delegation traveled from Skopje to Tirana. The role of Albania in the dynamics of the Kosovo and Macedonian conflicts is complex. On the one hand, as the national state of the Albanian people, Albania has an interest in the fate of ethnic Albanians across its borders and has functioned as an advocate of their interests. On the other hand, as a state undergoing a difficult internal transformation, its leadership has a strong interest in avoiding destabilization of the environment around Albania or the introduction of new and destabilizing forces into the country's domestic politics. Albania has been involved in the continuing conflict in Kosovo as an advocate of the interests of the ethnic Albanians there. The Albanian government has provided consistent diplomatic support for the Rugova parallel government. But the present leadership of Albania also has a strong interest in the peaceful resolution of that conflict. The creation of an independent Kosovo would have incalculable effects on the domestic politics of Albania. The prospect that Kosovar Albanians might seek union with Albania would likely ignite north-south cleavages in Albania with similarly incalculable consequences. Thus, the current Albanian leadership appears to be attempting to steer a course between support for Kosovar aspirations and support for stabilizing existing international relationships.

The delegation heard several variations of a single theme on Kosovo during its visit to Tirana. This theme focused on restoring to Kosovo the level of autonomy it enjoyed in 1974, plus more, as a means of resolving the conflict there. In some cases, this formula was presented as an interim solution, while in others it was presented as a "solution." President Sali Berisha argued that "Kosovo cannot have less than it had in 1974." But he also hinted that the rights embodied in the 1974 Yugoslav constitution might be merely a way station on the road to independence. "If the Albanians of Kosovo had the 1974 rights now," he argued, "their independence from Belgrade would have developed faster."

Berisha emphasized that the Kosovo problem would have to be resolved through negotiations and that "Albania will encourage [the Kosovar leadership] to negotiate." He also underscored the fact that Rugova is "a real president with a real mandate" and therefore the rightful Kosovar representative. Negotiations, he added, have to take place "in the presence of a third party." The consistent message received by the delegation throughout the region was that only the United States could play this role.

Minister of Defense Safet Zhulali began his assessment of the current security situation by describing the Albanian people as "a people who were divided a long time ago into two states with a geographic and ethnic continuity." In his view those two states are Albania and Kosovo. In Macedonia, he argued, participation of the Albanians in the government is a satisfactory outcome. In Kosovo that would not be enough. His support for negotiations was only lukewarm. ("Perhaps the beginning of a dialogue will be possible.") And his evaluation of the Kosovars did not suggest much enthusiasm for a "1974-plus" scenario:

> Kosovars recognize that they are part of Serbia. They will not like this, but they will accept a step-by-step approach. They will never accept being part of Serbia, but I think a step-by-step realization of this can lead to the solution of this problem.

The contradictions inherent in this statement are characteristic of many of the statements we heard in Tirana (and elsewhere). They reflect the competing, even conflicting aspirations of many of the Albanians we interviewed throughout the region: the desire for individual freedom and equality for Albanians in Kosovo (and in Macedonia) on the one hand, and the nationalist aspiration to independence for Kosovo, on the other.

Deputy Foreign Minister Arjan Starova expressed a clear interest in achieving some positive movement on the Kosovo issue and a willingness to support less than independence, but not less than 1974 status. Kosovo, he argued, must be recognized as having the right to self-determination. Even this outcome had to be understood as an interim solution, not the end of the process. The speaker of the parliament, Pjeter Arbnori, declared very simply that "I am for a step-by-step solution with a return to the constitution of 1974 as the first step, but with a guarantee that these [1974] rights will not be weakened but will be strengthened." Edward Selami, the chairman of the parliamentary foreign affairs committee, expressed essentially the same position in a separate meeting.

The 1974 constitutional arrangements that were referred to so many times during our meetings in Albania were either misrepresented or misunderstood in the same way as they were by LDK leaders in Prishtina. Our Albanian interlocutors also displayed a similar imprecision about the history of Kosovo. One parliamentary leader, for example, insisted that "Kosovo is a matter of ex-Yugoslavia, not Serbia," while another simply stated that "Kosovo was never part of Serbia."

One way to reconcile the many versions of the "1974-plus" argument heard during the delegation's visit to the region is to conceive of a solution in which Kosovo is elevated to the status of a republic equal to Serbia and Montenegro but remains a part of the FRY. The delegation discussed this option throughout our mission. But it is an option that is highly controversial among Albanian leaders.[11]

The "third republic" option represents a means by which to increase Kosovar autonomy while preserving international borders. President Berisha was very clear about his support for the preservation of existing borders. But opinions in Albania do differ on this issue. The Socialist (former Communist) Party leaders with whom we met stated rather matter-of-factly that union of Albania and Kosovo "is desirable" and that "this is a nation divided in two." These leaders were careful to distinguish between Kosovo, which they defined as part of the Albanian national question, and Macedonia, where they defined the issue as one of equal rights within the existing state.

The general population, journalists reported, is largely passive on the Kosovo issue. They suggested that Kosovo is a more sensitive issue in the north and that attitudes toward Kosovars were negative in Tirana. Attitudes in Tirana, they suggested, reflected the fact that Kosovars had been involved in certain economic activities in the city that resulted in losses for the local population in the period immediately following the end of communism. One of the country's parliamentary leaders reported during a more informal discussion that the population in the south tends to oppose union with Kosovo.

Mass perceptions of the Kosovo issue are complicated by cultural and political cleavages among the Albanians. Albanian Catholics in northern Albania share a cultural and literary tradition distinct from that of the south. The Kosovars, although themselves also northerners and ethnoculturally Geg, have been the political and cultural allies of Tirana, which has imposed a unified literary language on the country based on the language of southern Albania and its ethno-culturally Tosk population. The Kosovars aligned themselves with Tirana and the Tosk-based unified language, officially adopting it for themselves in 1968–72. The decision to do so can be seen as a conscious effort on the part of the Kosovar leadership to promote unity between the Albanians of Kosovo and Albania.

The cultural differences between the Tosks of the south and the Gegs of the north also have political dimensions. Much of the leadership of the Communist period was drawn from the south, while the postcommunist leadership is from the north. The involvement of the Kosovars in Albanian politics thus threatens to tip the political balance in contemporary Albanian politics in favor of the south and stoke cultural resentments in the north.

The Kosovo issue thus has the potential to split the Albanian electorate along a north-south cleavage. Some Albanian politicians used Kosovo as a campaign issue in the May 1996 elections. For President Berisha, some positive movement toward a negotiated solution would be very helpful in shoring up his political prestige, badly damaged by the unfairly manipulated elections in May and his subsequent repression of protest.

Our discussions in Albania were marked by a tendency among Albanian elites to interpret the Dayton agreement as de facto partition of Bosnia-Herzegovina and as a precedent for Kosovo. President Berisha viewed Dayton as partition, as "recognition of a fait accompli of war," but rejected it as a precedent for the partition of Kosovo. He argued that partition of Kosovo itself would leave one-third of Kosovo in Serbia and lead to partition of Macedonia. He suggested that Kosovo could become independent while Macedonia remained whole, alleging that Macedonian territorial integrity depends more on Bulgaria than on Kosovo. In effect, President Berisha was arguing that Kosovo already constitutes a distinct entity akin to Macedonia by virtue of its status in the former Yugoslavia. From this perspective, granting international status to Kosovo would amount to recognition of an existing border and would not call into question the territorial integrity of Macedonia.

The treatment of Macedonia by officials in Tirana was characterized by several indications of the low priority they assign to Macedonia as a state. Albanian leaders, like the ethnic Albanian elites in Macedonia itself, showed a marked tendency to overstate the size of the ethnic Albanian population of Macedonia. They also challenged, directly or indirectly, the distinctiveness of Macedonian national identity. All the senior officials with whom the delegation met declared their support for the existence of the Macedonian state but pressed for an expansion of the rights of Albanians within it. All supported the right of Albanians to use their own language in the media, in government, and in higher education. Some advanced the argument that Albanians constituted a "state-forming element" in Macedonia, which implies support for the demands for constitutional change advanced by ethnic Albanian leaders in Macedonia. But it was clear from our discussions that Macedonia represented a far less urgent issue for the Albanian elite and commanded far less of their attention than did Kosovo.

Negotiation of a solution to the Kosovo question must involve the LDK. Ultimately, the political leadership of Albania will play an important supporting role, but only a supporting role. Even if multiple political voices are heard from Kosovo, and the LDK alone cannot guarantee the success of a negotiation, it is clear that no agreement can be implemented over the objections of the LDK. That is why the views expressed to the delegation by a senior member of the LDK's parallel "Government of the Republic of Kosova" are of such importance. He informed the delegation that "1974" is acceptable as a starting point for negotiations, because "we are not so fanatical as to demand independence immediately." The greater flexibility inherent in this position can be attributed directly to the impact of the Dayton agreement. He argued that events in "former Bosnia-Herzegovina" demonstrate that those who use force are rewarded. Because the LDK has no military power, it must show flexibility. He acknowledged that Kosovo had had a dual status under the old regime: it was part of Serbia but also participated at the federal level as the de facto equal of Serbia and the other republics, at least for most questions. But he insisted that in exchange for accepting "1974" as a starting point, "we ask for the other side to recognize that the former Yugoslavia no longer exists." Negotiations between the two sides would then focus on defining a new relationship between them. In the interim, international guarantees would be necessary to ensure implementation of "1974." Negotiations would have to take place "in the presence of a mediator, a serious one." The latter amounted to the only "precondition" he attached to such talks, but it is a difficult one to surmount in view of Serbian objections.

The positions expressed by Albanian political leaders in Tirana are consistent with those expressed by this Kosovar leader, as well as the more pragmatic unofficial views expressed in Belgrade. They also are consistent with the views of Macedonian government officials and of more pragmatic Macedonian and ethnic Albanian political leaders. All these views converge around the idea of negotiating a short-term modus vivendi in Kosovo consisting of some form of autonomy that could be described as "1974 plus." This modus vivendi would permit the conduct of longer-term negotiations over a more lasting solution to the Kosovo question. An interim solution within the framework of the FRY would contribute to reducing tensions in Macedonia. Encouragement and support from the political leadership of Albania for negotiations within the frameworks of the FRY and the existing Macedonian state would make a significant contribution to strengthening the position of ethnic Albanian leaders in Kosovo and Macedonia who embark on such a strategy and help protect them against the inevitable attacks of more extreme nationalists within their own communities.

OBSERVING THE OBSERVERS

LANGUAGE, ETHNICITY, AND POWER IN THE 1994
MACEDONIAN CENSUS AND BEYOND

VICTOR A. FRIEDMAN

In Sarajevo, before the Yugoslav war, there was a museum at one end of the bridge where Archduke Ferdinand was assassinated.[1] Among the displays at this museum was a political cartoon from the period shortly before the outbreak of the Great War. The cartoon shows a disorderly circle of powder kegs, some with long, dangling fuses, others on their sides with gunpowder spilling out. In the center of the circle formed by these powder kegs are a few thin, ill-shaven, dark-mustachioed men in national costumes of the Balkan nations looking around bewildered. Standing outside the circle, eagerly extending lit matches to them, are plump, pale, well-groomed men in the West European formal dress of the Great Powers. Thus was the concept of "Balkan powder keg" understood in former Yugoslavia.[2] There is a certain irony in the image of the Balkans in the center and the Great Powers at the periphery, since in fact precisely the opposite is and has been the case in virtually every sphere of relations between southeastern Europe and the rest of that continent. And Macedonia became and remains a potential center of conflict because it is on the periphery of all its neighbors, who are themselves on the periphery of Europe.[3] During the nineteenth and early twentieth centuries, national movements in Albania, Bulgaria, Greece, and Serbia all crystallized in such a way that Macedonia was (and is) at the edge of their overlapping claims. One way that conflict has been expressed is through rival census claims.

In comparison to the current position of Albania and Kosovo, the Republic of Macedonia is both central and liminal. Unlike Kosovo with its shadow government and parallel education system, Macedonia meets the normal requirements for an independent country, but unlike Albania with its unequivocal international status and membership in the United Nations under its own name, Macedonia does not enjoy the normal recognition of an independent European state insofar as only some countries have recognized it under it own constitutional name, while others use the temporary United Nations term "Former Yugoslav Republic of Macedonia (FYROM)." Kosovo can be viewed as a region where an ethnolinguistic Serbian minority dominates the Albanian majority; Albania is a country ruled by its ethnolinguistic majority.[4] But in Macedonia, which has foreign troops stationed inside its borders (the U.S. and Nordic battalions of the United Nations Preventive Deployment in Macedonia), the very legitimacy of the identity of the majority ethnolinguistic group, that is, the Macedonians, is still subjected to equivocation, both purposeful and naive.[5] Moreover, some actors would dispute whether the Macedonians constitute a majority, or even a plurality, in the Republic of Macedonia. Although in many respects the situation of Albanian majorities in both Albania and Kosovo can be viewed as economically or politically worse than the situation of the Albanian minority in Macedonia, it is Macedonia that is arguably the most unstable of the three, the country on which Albanian and Kosovar attention is focused. One expression of the instability in Macedonia is the persistence of conflicting population figures.

CENSUSES: THE POLITICS OF COUNTING

The counting of populations has been potentially fraught with political tension for millennia. The Book of Numbers (I:2-3) describes a census for the purpose of preparing for war, and the census mentioned in the Gospel of Luke (II:1-5) was quite probably connected with Roman efforts at consolidating hegemony in what was then still the kingdom (but later the province) of Judea.[6] From June 21 until mid-July 1994, under intense internal and external political pressure, an extraordinary census took place in the Republic of Macedonia—the ordinary census having been conducted in 1991, when the republic was still "socialist" and a part of what is now former Yugoslavia. The 1994 census was not funded by the government of the country, as is ordinarily the case with modern censuses in sovereign states, but by international organizations—the Council of Europe (CE), which at that time still refused to admit the Republic of Macedonia, and the European Union (EU), whose policies toward Macedonia have often been dominated by Greece. The extraordinary census of 1994 thus provides an opportunity to view more broadly both the complexity of the Macedonian scene and the role of European mediation.[7] The 1994 Macedonian census raises fundamental issues of which the more recent conflicts such as those over education and language use at the republic level are continuations, and it is thus worthy of a more detailed account as a historical moment around which national and international tensions crystallized. Whatever the developments in Macedonia's future, the 1994 census is one of the key links in the chain of events leading to it. In this chapter, I examine the 1994 Macedonian census both as an event in itself, and as a part of the larger context of quests for identity and hegemony in the Balkans. In so doing, I hope to shed light not only on specific and general questions connected with the concepts of ethnic, linguistic, and religious identity, but also on the relationship of the supranational to the national, of the central to the marginal, and of "Europe" to the land mass west of the Urals and north of the Mediterranean. I suggest that the Western Powers, which to a great extent determine (and fund) the policies of the those actors designated as the international community, have continued to marginalize Macedonia by imposing their own constructs. These efforts have not contributed to the stabilization of Macedonia.

I was working in summer 1994 as a senior policy and political analyst covering Macedonia for the analysis and assessment unit organized by Susan Woodward for Yasushi Akashi, the Special Representative of the Secretary General, attached to the United Nations Protection Forces (UNPROFOR) stationed in former Yugoslavia. In connection with these duties, I arranged to be authorized as an outside observer of the extraordinary 1994 census in my capacity as a member of an international organization in accordance with article 33 of the census law. Although I was not officially connected with any of the census's funding organizations, the majority of their representatives were quite willing to allow me to accompany them on their duties and attend their meetings. As a result, I was able to observe both the process of the census and the European observers who were officially observing it.

Questions of ethnic identity, citizenship, language rights, and the interrelationships of the concepts of language, religion, and "nationality" were hotly contested in Macedonia. The census was therefore a clearly political event rather than the statistical exercise officials claimed it was. And this was not the first time that Macedonian census figures have been the subject of conflict concerning these factors. At the beginning of this century, as at the end, economic and political structures in the Balkans were unstable or in transition, wars were being fought, interethnic tensions were high, and Macedonia was the object of conflicting claims supported in part by conflicting census figures. Table A.1 displays examples of the figures that were used to bolster these claims to Macedonia at the end of the nineteenth and beginning of the twentieth centuries, as Ottoman power waned and the small states of southeastern Europe sought to consolidate and expand their respective hegemonies.

Although Dako in his book significantly entitled *Albania: The Master Key to the Near East* cites similar figures and refers to the obvious discrepancies as "amusing," these discrepancies are not entirely arbitrary.[8] Rather, at least to some extent, different authors of articles and books making nationalist arguments have selected criteria that would support their points of view.

In the case of Greek and Turkish authors, the choice was based on religion, schooling, or both. Any member of the Greek Orthodox Church, or, after 1870, any Patriarchist, as well as anyone who went to a Greek school (and because schooling was controlled by religion, Macedonian Christians were left with little choice until the mid-nineteenth century) was counted by the Greeks as a Greek. This practice gave rise to expressions such as "slavophone Greek" and "albanophone Greek."[9] The complete absence of Albanians from the Greek figures is explained by their being counted as Turks, Greeks, or miscellaneous on the basis of religion (Muslim, Orthodox, Catholic).[10]

Because the Serbian Orthodox Church and Serbian schools remained relatively weak except in parts of the north and west of Macedonia, Serbian authors selected specific isoglosses, that is, dialect boundaries based on individual linguistic features, to justify ethnic and therefore territorial claims, as illustrated in Table A.2 (see page 86) and Figure A.1 (see page 86).[11]

TABLE A.1[1]
CONFLICTING CENSUS FIGURES FOR MACEDONIA 1889–1905

ETHNIC GROUP	BULGARIAN	%	SERBIAN	%	GREEK	%	TURKISH	%
Bulgarians	1,181,336	52.31	57,600	2.01	332,162	19.26	896,497	30.80
Serbians	700	0.03	2,048,320	71.35	0	0.00	100,000	3.40
Greeks	228,702	10.13	201,140	7.01	652,795	37.85	307,000	10.60
Albanians	128,711	5.70	165,620	5.77	0	0.00	0	0.00
Turks	499,204	22.11	231,400	8.06	634,017	36.76	1,508,507	51.80[2]
Others	219,571	9.72	166,540	13.86	105,844	6.13	99,000	3.40
TOTAL	2,258,224	100.00	2,870,620	100.00	1,724,818	100.00	2,911,004	100.00

[1]The Bulgarian figures are from 1900, the Serbian from 1889, and the Greek from 1904. These are cited together in Baron d'Estournelles de Constant et al., *Report of the International Commission to Inquire into the Causes and Conduct of the Balkan Wars*, Division of Intercourse and Education, Publication no. 4, Washington, D.C.: Carnegie Endowment for International Peace, 1914 (reprinted 1993 as *The Other Balkan Wars* with an introduction by George Kennan), pp. 28–30, and represent those of the three states that were independent, had territorial claims to Macedonia, and fought one another over those claims in the Second Balkan War in 1913. I have added a Turkish account of the 1905 Ottoman census figures for comparison (Osman Yavuz Saral, *Kaybettiğimiz Rumeli* [Istanbul: Boğazici, 1975], p. 152). The Greek figures omit the sandžak of Skopje (Üsküp, vilayet of Kosovo [spuriously hellenized as Kossyphopedion in Cleanthes Nicolaides, *La Macédoine* (Berlin: Stuhr, 1899), p. 25, while the Bulgarian figures include the kaza of Tetovo (Kalkan-delen, sandžak of Prizren, vilayet of Kosovo) and the kazas of Debar (Dibre-i bâlâ) and Reka (Rikkalar/Zir Nanice) in the sandžaks of the vilayets of Salonika and Bitola/Monastir belonging to geographic Macedonia. For ease of comparison, I have added percentages. The selection from d'Estournelles de Constant was chosen because it is both typical of the discrepancies and because the republication of this report in 1993 has given it greater currency in the present situation. The category "Other" includes "Wallachians" (i.e., Romance-speakers now known as Vlahs and including Arumanians and Megleno-Romanians), Jews, Gypsies (modern Roms or Roma), "Miscellaneous" (Circassians, Armenians, etc.). For a Greek view of the period that refers to other sources, see Christopher J. Christides, *The Macedonian Camouflage in the Light of Facts and Figures* (Athens: Hellenic Publishing Co., 1949), pp. 32–33. See also Stephen Clissold, *A Short History of Yugoslavia: From Early Times to 1966* (Cambridge: Cambridge University Press, 1968), p. 136 for additional viewpoints. For figures relating to the postwar period, see Tošo Popovski, *Makedonskoto malcinstvo vo Bugarija, Grcija i Albanija* (Skopje: Makedonska kniga, 1981), pp. 187, 192–93, 247.

[2]Saral does not distinguish Turks from Albanians but writes: "Muslim (the majority Turkish, the minority Albanian)." The only other ethnic group listed in Saral's figures (included here as "Other" for ease of comparison) is "Wallachian" (p. 152).

TABLE A.2
Differing Isoglosses Used to Support Conflicting Territorial Claims
[1] The Reflex of Common Slavic *tj   **[2] The Presence of a Definite Article**

	[1] Shoulders	[2] Woman/The Woman
Serbian	pleći	žena
Macedonian	pleḱi	žena/ženata
Bulgarian	plešti	žena/ženata

Note: The forms cited in the table are those used in the modern standard languages. The dialectal situation is considerably more complicated but is irrelevant to the basic point being illustrated.

FIGURE A.1
Map Showing Approximate Locations of Isoglosses [1] and [2]

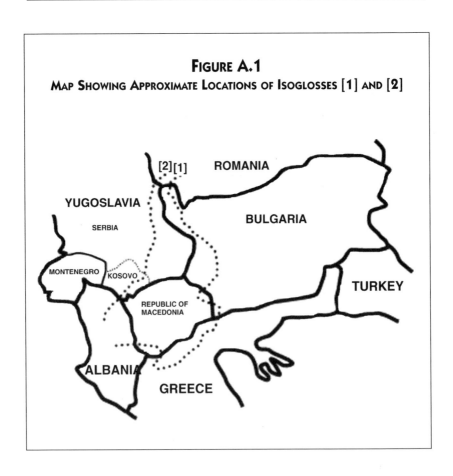

The isogloss illustrated by column one—the reflex of Common Slavic *tj, where Serbian and Macedonian have a single palatal stop or affricate rather than a combination of palatal fricative plus affricate or stop—was used by Belić to justify Serbian claims to virtually all of northern and central Macedonia.[12] Belić, citing Meillet, writes that the Macedonian dialects are neither Serbian nor Bulgarian and that politics will determine the linguistic fate of Macedonia. He then goes on to claim, however, on the basis of this single isogloss, that the north and central Macedonian dialects are basically Serbian while the south is basically Bulgarian. Belić ridicules Bulgarian scholars who were claiming all of Macedonian as well as Southern Serbian as Bulgarian dialects by suggesting that his opinion coincided with that of impartial European scholarship, that is, his interpretation of Meillet.[13] He declared that, because Serbia had contact with the West while Bulgaria "slept deeply under the Turkish yoke," the resulting difference in intellectual development could not easily be overcome. The genuinely impartial French scholar Vaillant, however, observes that Belić's argument is based on one phonetic trait and that most Slavists agree that Macedonian is actually a part of a Macedo-Bulgarian group that has been subjected to the prolonged influence of Serbian.[14] He lists numerous phonological traits that link Macedonian with Bulgarian rather than with Serbian.[15] Vaillant concludes that Macedonian is not a dialect of Bulgarian but deserves a separate place in the Macedo-Bulgarian group.[16] It is important to note that Vaillant wrote six years before the political recognition of Macedonian as an independent language

At the same time, choosing a feature such as the presence of the postposed definite article—as in the second column of Table A.2—helped justify Bulgarian territorial claims to the Timok-Morava valley in southern Serbia as well as to Macedonia.[17] Bulgarian figures assumed that virtually any Slav in Macedonia was Bulgarian; the numbers were also inflated by assuming higher fertility and incidence of extended families for Slavs than for other groups.[18] Thus, for example, if a given village had fifty Albanian houses and forty Slavic houses, by counting five members per Albanian household and seven members per Slavic household based on the foregoing assumption, we end up with a Slavic majority despite the smaller number of houses: 280 Slavs as opposed to 250 Albanians. This is an early example of how important statistical and demographic assumptions underlying counting procedures can be for the outcome of censuses; such assumptions continue to be characteristic of censuses to this day.

Notably absent from these statistics are any figures representing the views of ethnic Macedonians themselves.[19] In general, there is very little evidence of Macedonian views in the published literature except occasional moments.[20] As Rossos makes abundantly clear, the suppression of Macedonian ethnic identity in all its manifestations was in the interests not only of all the small powers that laid claim to the territory, but also of the great powers that supported the various small powers and that ultimately had a stake in maintaining the partition of Macedonia as a viable solution for peace.[21] Brown discusses heretofore untapped archival sources outside the Balkans that attest both to the existence of a separate sense of Macedonian nationality at the beginning of this century and to attempts to dismiss it.[22] In certain respects that situation is being replicated today, and population figures are again being used to bolster conflicting claims ranging from minority rights to irredentism. In particular, the technique of privileging religion over language as the basis of identity, which was used by both Turks and Greeks (and later Bulgarians and Serbs) to hegemonize and assimilate various populations in Macedonia, is again being brought into play, as will be seen below.

THE 1991 YUGOSLAV CENSUS IN MACEDONIA

During April 1–15, 1991, under conditions of impending political disintegration, the Socialist Federal Republic of Yugoslavia conducted its last census. Before the end of that year, while the census data were still being processed, war broke out in former Yugoslavia, and the Republic of Macedonia subsequently declared independence. The census itself was carried out in an atmosphere of distrust and animosity. Led by the two largest Albanian-identified political parties in Macedonia, the Party for Democratic Prosperity (PPD) and the smaller but more vocal and radical People's Democratic Party (PDP), the majority of Albanians in Macedonia (and elsewhere in Yugoslavia) boycotted the 1991 census, claiming that they would be purposefully undercounted.

The Party for Democratic Prosperity was founded on April 15, 1990, in Tetovo, now a predominantly Albanian town with close historical and communication links to Kosovo, which is just on the other side of Mount Šar.[23] Branches of the PPD continued to be founded in various towns throughout western Macedonia during that year. The PPD proclaimed protection of minority rights as its major goal, and indeed in the 1990 local elections, seven Turks and seven Muslims (presumably Slavic-speaking) were elected to local councils on its ticket.[24] Nonetheless, both the PPD and the PDP are basically Albanian rights parties that advocate treating Albanians not as a minority but as a "constitutive nation" in Macedonia.[25] The boycott was first called for by the Peoples Democratic Party and was observed in the communes (opštini) of Debar, Gostivar, Kičevo, Kumanovo, Ohrid, Skopje, Struga, Tetovo, and Titov Veles.[26] The bureau of statistics estimated the data for Albanians in the boycotted communes by means of statistical projections utilizing the data from the 1981 census, natural growth of the population during the intercensus period, migration, and other statistical data.[27] The preliminary results were published in November 1991. Table A.3 (see pages 90–91) gives comparative statistics for all the postwar censuses conducted in the territory of the Republic of Macedonia.[28] The categories "Egyptian" and "Bosniac" represent new sociopolitical realities.[29]

Before the preliminary figures for the 1991 census were published, Albanian political actors began an international media campaign declaring not merely that they had been miscounted, but that in fact Albanians constituted about 40 percent of the population of Macedonia, that is 700,000 to 800,000 people.[30] Albanian political actors were supported in their claim by Greece, which denies the existence of a Macedonian language and nationality altogether, particularly on its own territory.[31] Representatives of other groups also cited larger statistics: Serbs claimed up to 300,000, Turks up to 200,000, Roms 200,000, Greeks 250,000, and Ĝupci, Bulgarians, and Vlahs about 30,000 each.[32] Added together, these claims surpassed the total number of inhabitants of Macedonia, even without counting Macedonians. These claims clearly sacrificed statistical accuracy to an effort to gain political power and hegemony.

The Albanian public relations effort was successful. Within a year of the publication of the preliminary results of the 1991 Yugoslav census, Geert-Hinrich Ahrens, a German diplomat with the rank of ambassador and head of the Working Group for Human Rights and Minorities within the International Conference on Former Yugoslavia (ICFY), called for an extraordinary census in Macedonia to be supervised by the "international community."[33] Ambassador Ahrens made two proposals: One involved only those areas with large Albanian populations, the other concerned the entire country. Such a pair of proposals had many implications and repercussions. The first proposal focused on the Albanians to the exclusion of all the other minorities of Macedonia, which, according to the 1991 census made up 14.37 percent of the

Table A.3
Totals and Percentages for Declared Nationality (Narodnost) in all Post-World War II Censuses Conducted in the Republic of Macedonia

(Census total by year, number, and percentage (rounded upward where necessary))

Declared Nationality (narodnost)	1948	%	1953	%	1961	%	1971	%	1981	%	1991	%	1994[1]	%
Macedonians	789,548	68.5	860,699	66.0	1,000,854	71.2	1,142,375	69.3	1,279,323	67.0	1,328,187	65.3	1,288,330	66.5
Albanians	197,389	17.1	162,524	12.4	183,108	13.0	279,871	17.0	377,208	19.8	441,987	21.7	442,914	22.9
Turks	95,940	8.3	203,938	15.6	131,481	9.4	108,552	6.6	86,591	4.5	77,080	3.8	77,252	4.0
Roms[2]	19,500	1.7	20,462	1.6	20,606	1.5	24,505	1.5	43,125	2.3	52,103	2.6	43,732	2.3
Vlahs	9,511	0.8	8,668	0.6	8,046	0.6	7,190	0.6	6,384	0.3	7,764	0.4	8,467	0.4
Serbs	29,721	2.6	35,112	2.7	42,728	3.0	46,465	2.8	44,468	2.3	42,775	2.1	39,260	2.0
Muslims	1,560	0.1	1,591	0.1	3,002	0.2	1,248	0.1	39,513	2.1	31,356	1.5	15,315	0.8
Bulgarians	889	0.1	920	0.1	3,087	0.2	3,334	0.2	1,980	0.1	1,370	0.0	1,547	0.1
Greeks	–	–	848	–	836	0.1	536	0.0	707	0.1	474	0.0	349	0.0
Egyptian	–	–	–	–	–	–	–	–	–	--	3,307	0.2	3,169	0.2
Bosniac	–	–	–	–	–	–	–	–	–	–	–	–	7,244	0.4
Yugoslav	–	–	–	–	1,260	0.1	3,652	0.2	14,225	0.7	15,703	0.8	595[3]	0.0
Other[4]	8,928	0.8	9,752	0.8	10,995	0.7	29,580	1.7	15,612	0.8	31,858	1.6	8,703	0.4
Total	1,152,986	100	1,304,514	100	1,406,003	100	1,647,308	100	1,909,136	100	2,033,964	100	1,936,877	100

Sources: Svetlana Antonovska et al., Broj i struktura na naselenieto vo Republika Makedonija po opštini i nacionalna pripadnost: Sostojba 31.03.1991 godina (Skopje: Republički zavod za statistika, 1991); Statistički godišnik na Republika Makedonija 1993 (Skopje: Republički Zavod za Statistika, 1994); Popis '94: Podatoci za segašnosta i idninata. prvi rezultati. Soopštenie 1, Soopštenie 2 (Skopje: Republički Zavod za statistika, 1994); Ibrahim Latific et al., Vitalna, etnička i migraciona obeležja. Popis stanovništva 1961 (Belgrade: Savezni zavod za statistiku, 1970); Boro Pekevski et al., Naselenie po narodnost vo SR Makedonija. Popis na naselenieto i stanovite, 1971 god (Skopje: Republički zavod za statistika, 1973); Stanovništvo po narodosti (knj. 9): Konacni rezultati popisa stanovišta od 15 marta 1948 godine (Belgrade: Savezni zavod za statistiku, 1954); Statistički bilten broj 1295. Popis stanovništva domačinstva i stanova u 1981 godini: Nacionalni sastav stanovništva po opštinama (Belgrade: Savezni zavod za statistiku, 1981).

1. According to Dr. Svetlana Antonovska (personal communication, May 25, 1995), director of the Republic Bureau of Statistics, the lower figures for some nationalities in 1994 versus 1991 is due to the fact that citizens living abroad for more than one year were included in the 1991 census, whereas in the 1994 census—in accordance with international norms—only those citizens living abroad for one year or less were counted. The figures cited for 1994 are based on preliminary results available as of this writing (April 1996). The Republic Bureau of Statistics was scheduled to meet with the Group of Experts from June 18 to June 15, 1996 to produce the final result, which will be published subsequently.

2. The predominantly Romani-speaking ethnic group known as Gypsies in English and Cigani in Macedonian (similar ethnonyms are used in most of the languages of Central and Eastern Europe) is now referred to by the native ethnonym Rom (singular) in scholarly literature as well as official documents in many countries. (The term was official in the 1971 Yugoslav census.) Although in languages other than English this form has been unhesitatingly adapted to the grammar of the language in which it is used (for example, in Macedonian the plural of Rom is Romi), considerable inconsistency has arisen in English usage. Thus as the plural of Rom some scholars and other serious writers use the Romani form Roma, others adapt the word to English morphology and write Roms, others use a pluralized adjective Romanies, and some treat the noun as uninflected, using Rom for both singular and plural. I have argued elsewhere (Freidman and Hancock, 1995) that just as in English the plural of Turk is Turks and not Türkler, so the plural of Rom should be Roms and not Roma. I would argue that the form Roma exoticizes and marginalizes rather than emphasizes the fact that the group in question is an ethnic group just as are Turks, Magyars (not Magyarok), and so forth (to be sure, a unique ethnic group, but still an ethnic group). The usage in other European languages supports this view.

3. This figure includes those who declared "Yugoslav" as well as nationalities not counted separately in the census, mostly from Africa, East Asia, and the Middle East (MIC, January 5, 1995).

4. Yugoslav and Macedonian censuses distinguished up to 34 nationality categories as well as several other types including those who declared a regional identity and those who did not declare a nationality. For the sake of conciseness, I have grouped all the smaller categories, none of which are relevant for this paper, under the designation "Other." This designation includes the following specified groups: Austrian, Belgian, Croatian, Czech, Danish, Dutch, English, French, German, Hungarian, Italian, Jewish, Montenegrin, Norwegian, Polish, Romanian, Russian, Rusyn, Slovak, Slovenian, Swiss, Swedish, and Ukrainian. This category also includes intellectuals who protested the use of nationality as a classification by making facetious declarations, among which the most popular were "lightbulb" and "refrigerator" (personal communication, Robert Hayden, University of Pittsburgh).

population. It gave implicit legitimacy to Albanian claims for special treatment, in addition to legitimizing Albanian politicians' right to claim discrimination and to demand a recount, as it were. At the same time, the proposals helped reify as a Macedonian-Albanian conflict tensions that had been building since the riots in Kosovo in 1981 but that were not an inherent feature of Macedonian life at all periods.

THE 1994 "EUROPEAN" CENSUS IN MACEDONIA

Ahrens' announcement of November 1992 was followed by nineteen months of uninterrupted dispute. First there was an intense controversy over whether or not to hold the census.[34] This agreed upon, there followed prolonged debate over the wording of the census law, which was eventually passed with the support of the Albanian members of parliament. One of the chief issues was language use in the census, and article 35 of the census law provided for bilingual forms in Albanian, Turkish, Romani, Vlah, and Serbian in addition to Macedonian.[35] Finally, just as the census was actually beginning, there were serious behind-the-scenes negotiations with the Albanian members of parliament, who threatened to call for a boycott, despite the presence of observers from the International Census Observation Mission (ICOM) and the expense incurred by the European organizations.

The overseers of the census appointed by the European organizations were officially called the Group of Experts.[36] Their fields of expertise, however, did not include knowledge pertaining to Macedonia. Rather they were, for the most part, statisticians and bureaucrats without previous Balkan experience.[37] Many members of the ICOM team, including some of the highest ranking, told me that they were quite surprised when they discovered that they were embroiled in highly charged political issues, as opposed to a mechanical statistical exercise, and they expressed confusion and dismay over the complex ethnic situation they encountered. In view of the origins of the 1994 Macedonian census described above as well as explicit statements by Albanian political actors, the event was clearly linked to a political issue, namely the claim of Albanian politicians for special (nonminority) status for Albanians within Macedonia based on their large numbers.[38] The Group of Experts, however, attempted to avoid the impression that it was involving itself in the internal political affairs of a sovereign state by publicly declaring that the census was merely a statistical exercise. It can be argued that by labeling the leadership of ICOM the "Group of

Experts" while avoiding the direct involvement of anyone familiar with Macedonia, the CE was attempting to lay claim to adjudicating authority in Macedonian internal affairs and at the same time project an image of objectivity.[39]

The lack of knowledge of Macedonia on the part of the CE and ICOM was given symbolic representation in the orientation packet for members of the ICOM team. The only item relating to the country itself rather than ICOM's mission in it, was a chart listing Cyrillic printed and cursive letters with the names of the letters in Cyrillic and Latin orthography and labeled simply "L'alphabet." The very lack of a qualifying adjective in a sense erases Macedonian from the observer's view, and in fact the chart was not a guide to Macedonian Cyrillic, but a table of Russian Cyrillic with the last six letters blanked out. Although the last six letters of Russian Cyrillic do not occur in Macedonian, seven other letters that are used in Macedonian Cyrillic but not in Russian were missing from the chart.[40] To compound the effect, the names of the Russian Cyrillic letters utilize a vowel whose letter comes at the end of the alphabet, so the names of the letters used a symbol that was not given in the list of letters. This chart not only embodied the lack of concern with which the CE and ICOM approached the Macedonian context in which it presumed to operate, but also gave false information to the purveyors of expert knowledge. In focusing on the Albanian question, ICOM lost sight of the Macedonian one.

Similarly, the privileging of Albanian claims over all others was symbolically represented on the ICOM observers' control forms for censused households.[41] Although the Macedonian control forms had sections for indicating the six ethnic affiliations defined by the languages of the census forms, as did the ICOM control form on enumerators, the ICOM household control form specified only Macedonian and Albanian, the remainder being subsumed under "Others." The difference in these forms gave written representation to the different conceptions of ICOM and the Macedonian government concerning the purpose of the census.

On the first day of the census, June 21, 1994, I attended a press conference given by Ambassador Ahrens of ICFY, Werner Haug, chairman of the Group of Experts, and Robin Guthrie, director of Social and Economic Affairs, Council of Europe. In addition to insisting to those assembled that the census was a statistical exercise with no political dimension, the expert team focused on Albanian objections to question 6 on form p-1, citizenship, for which the four possible answers were Macedonian, alien, person without citizenship, and pending status

(*vo tek*). The chief problem was that, despite assurances to the contrary, the Ministry of Internal Affairs (MVR) had not succeeded in dis-
tributing all citizenship documents by the time the census began. In
Eastern Macedonia that was not particularly important. Thus, for example, in Radoviš the local government actually used census enumerators
to help distribute citizenship documents. Although the problems of
document distribution occurred throughout Macedonia, Albanians
maintained that a disproportionately high number of qualified
Albanians were without citizenship documents. This problem was complicated by the number of Albanians who had fled oppression in Kosovo
but whose status in Macedonia was unregulated. Although a compromise solution was eventually reached, a special MVR form tabulating
citizenship was added on July 2 in three group areas, and the ICOM mission was upset at this irregularity.[42]

After the press conference, I attended a separate meeting between
members of the Group of Experts and a group of PPD members headed
by Abdurahman Aliti, who later became president of the PPD. The
topic was the threatened last-minute boycott mentioned above. Guthrie
spoke in very strong terms to Aliti about the need for his party to cooperate with the census. Aliti unhappily noted that in reality the census
did indeed have a political dimension, and that if he or his party openly called for support of the census they would be wiped off the political
map. (Although Aliti did not state who would do this, the PDP or radicals in the PPD would have been the only logical candidates.) He said
that the best his party could do was promise not to actually call for a
boycott, but neither would they call for support of the census. Aliti
made it clear that he understood the situation and wanted to see the
census work, but he stated that he also saw no point in allowing radicals
to destroy his political career. I then accompanied the experts to their
offices at the Bureau of Statistics, where the citizenship question was
again the main order of business. Because no one on the ICOM team
knew either Macedonian or Albanian, they were at a disadvantage
when a question of the wording of the rules concerning the citizenship
question arose, and the only rule book available was in Macedonian.
Members of ICOM also told me that they began their mission with no
idea of its political implications or the tremendous ethnic and cultural
complexity of the region. They thought they were going to be oversee-
ing the technical aspects of a statistical exercise.

At the end of that first day, the Group of Experts' discussion about
the complications they had encountered also revealed their view of
Macedonia as something other than European. One member of the

group joked that they should conduct the census like the one 2,000 years ago, when everyone went to his or her native village, a reference to the Gospel of Luke mentioned at the beginning of this paper. The unintended irony of her comment was that this was precisely what the Macedonians would have wanted and what the Albanians would have feared, because an indeterminate number of Albanians had come to Macedonia from Kosovo and elsewhere since World War II, especially since the Kosovo uprising of 1981. The citizenship law set the term of residence at fifteen years, which had the effect of excluding the most recent wave of Albanian immigration. During the debate over this law, Macedonian nationalist politicians advocated a term of thirty years; Albanian politicians pressed for five years. The longer term would have excluded the majority of Albanians who had come to Macedonia from Kosovo.[43] Another member of the team, speaking in French, described how the census was conducted in Turkey, where there was a curfew (in French, *couvre-feu*), requiring everyone to stay indoors and await the census takers under penalty of a heavy fine. A British member of the team misunderstood the French and thought the Turks burned villages during their census. In both the joke and the misunderstanding, the Balkans in general and Macedonia in particular emerge as a primitive "other," backward or barbaric.

It was at the beginning of another meeting between the Group of Experts and Albanian political leaders the following morning that I asked Ambassador Ahrens if it might not be the case that ethnic tensions were in fact exacerbated by internationalizing Albanian claims in Macedonia via the CE/ICFY-sponsored census.[44] Dr. Ahrens responded that he thought the international intervention was beneficial and cited as evidence the fact that as soon as the CE agreed to fund the census, Albanian claims dropped immediately from 40 percent to 30 percent. Indeed, during the negotiations that I attended, at which Albanian politicians were expressing particular misgivings over the issue of citizenship, the figure they cited as being the minimum below which they would claim falsification was 25 percent. I should note that even before the first results were released, the percentage claimed had jumped, and after the first results were published, and despite ICOM approval, the figure 40 percent was again being cited (Albanian prime minister Alexander Meksi, for example, reportedly cited the figure 800,000).[45]

At times ICOM approached the Macedonian government with a seriously distrustful, almost adversarial attitude. Because the 1994 census was being conducted as a result of the Albanian boycott of the 1991 census, there was a tendency at ICOM to view Albanian claims as based in fact rather than raising an unresolved question. Thus ICOM sometimes viewed the Macedonian government as guilty unless proven innocent. Censuses conducted by sovereign states are not normally overseen by other organizations, while censuses in colonies are supervised by their colonial rulers. The fact that the 1994 census in the Republic of Macedonia was conducted under pressure from and with funding from external organizations put that country in an ambiguous position. On the one hand, the external funding and oversight by individuals who were not citizens of Macedonia put the country in a position similar to that of a nonsovereign entity. On the other hand, Macedonia was treated as a sovereign state engaged in discriminatory behavior. The following incident shows how ICOM's lack of preparation combined with its tendency to view the Macedonian government with distrust led to incorrect judgments. In July I was approached by ICOM members who informed me that the government was discriminating against Muslims by not listing them as Bosniacs (Bošnjaci) or by not giving their language as Serbo-Croatian. These ICOM members had been in contact with Bosniac political activists who had tried to convince them that all Slavic Muslims in Macedonia are Serbo-Croatian-speaking, Bosniac, or both. When I responded that there was a significant number of Macedonian-speaking Muslims—popularly known as Torbeš, although they prefer to be called Muslimani—who do not speak Serbo-Croatian and who do not identify as Bosniac, the ICOM reaction was a combination of surprise and skepticism. In the end they came to understand that the situation was indeed as I had explained it to them, but the very fact that such a misunderstanding could arise demonstrates not only the distrust toward the Macedonians with which the European experts approached the census but also their difficulty in distinguishing information from misinformation disseminated by some ethnopolitical actors.

Macedonian Muslims often live in underdeveloped, neglected, and isolated areas, such as the municipalities of Debar and Kičevo, where there is no ethnic absolute majority. They have therefore been vulnerable to manipulation by Albanian and Turkish politicians who have convinced some of them that they are Slavicized Albanians or Turks rather than Islamicized Slavs and that they could therefore rely more on Turkish or Albanian political parties to support their economic interests, because in economies of shortage such interests tend to fragment along ethnic lines.[46] The emphasis of Macedonian nationalist politicians on the connection between the Macedonian Orthodox Church and

Macedonian nationality has further alienated some Macedonian Muslims.[47] Census attempts in Macedonian-speaking Muslim villages ran into cases where a monolingual Macedonian Muslim family would demand a bilingual Albanian or Turkish form with an interpreter but then have to have the Albanian or Turkish translated into Macedonian. These incidents·were part of a larger pattern of conscious language shift based on religion, such as the incident in the monolingual Macedonian Muslim village of Bačište (Kičevo municipality), where parents demanded an Albanian school for their children.[48]

A general problem with the 1994 Macedonian census, as with other European censuses, was the definition of the categories "mother tongue" and "nationality" (the ICOM control forms used "ethnic affiliation" and "national affiliation" interchangeably). The concepts of ethnicity, nationality, language, and religion have a complex history of interrelationships in Macedonia, one whose complexity continues today. Thus, for example, some Muslim speakers of Macedonian declare their nationality as Albanian or Turkish on the basis of identifying their religion with Turkish or Albanian ethnicity. Similarly, some Christian speakers of Albanian declare their nationality as Macedonian by equating Macedonian Orthodox Christianity with Macedonian ethnicity. As might be expected, Albanian ethnopoliticians insist that Macedonian-identified Albanian-speakers are Albanians, while Macedonians insist that Albanian-identified Macedonian speakers are Macedonians. There was also the citizenship-based category Yugoslav, which until 1991 was steadily growing in popularity among both Slavs and non-Slavs. Now that Macedonia is no longer part of Yugoslavia, however, this category has ceased to be valid for most people, because it refers to another country.[49]

At least some ICOM observers were unaware of the difference between Serbo-Croatian and Macedonian when they arrived to observe the census, as reflected in their questions to me. When they finally grasped that the difference was a linguistic one, they concluded that language was therefore the basis of nationality. While language and ethnic or national affiliation coincide to a certain extent in Macedonia, such is clearly not always the case, as can be seen not only from such categories as "Muslim" but also from Table A.4 (see page 98), which gives statistics for the correspondence between declared nationality and declared mother tongue for the 1953 and 1981 censuses (figures for 1994 have not yet been processed).

By attempting to impose a West European construct equating language with nationality (and nationality with statehood), ICOM helped

TABLE A.4
DIFFERENCE BETWEEN DECLARED NATIONALITY AND DECLARED MOTHER TONGUE
FOR THE SIX MAIN LANGUAGES OF THE REPUBLIC OF MACEDONIA: 1953 AND 1981

DECLARED NATIONALITY	DECLARED MOTHER TONGUE					
	MACEDONIAN	ALBANIAN	TURKISH	SERBO-CROAT	ROMANI	VLAH
1953						
Macedonians	853,971	1,986	281	934	277	2,565
Albanians	2,152	153,502	6,569	181	70	1
Turks	32,392	27,087	143,615	534	70	10
Roms	1,040	860	2,066	25	16,456	1
Vlahs	137	4	2	14	0	8,130
Serbs	3,945	0	8	31,070	41	9
Muslim	*	*	*	*	*	*
Yugoslav	2,152	25	50	563	2	4
Other	322	341	569	5,258	173	31
Total	**896,651**	**183,805**	**153,160**	**38,579**	**17,089**	**10,751**
1981						
Macedonians	1,276,878	190	160	547	316	*
Albanians	1,218	374,181	3	440	1,697	*
Turks	16,608	8,592	60,768	366	94	*
Roms	4,160	1,697	808	24	36,399	*
Vlahs	1,111	1	0	3	2	5,257
Serbs	8,521	10	3	35,867	14	*
Muslim	15,075	4,968	2,038	16,325	308	30
Yugoslav	7,645	1,943	274	2,746	530	*
Other	13,282	4,247	2,853	17,031	1,280	*
Total	**1,334,498**	**391,829**	**64,907**	**63,349**	**37,780**	**5,931**

*Not specified

Sources: Savezni Zavod za statistiku, Stanovništvo po narodnosti (Knj. 9): Konačni rezultati popisa stanovništva od 15 marta 1948 godine (Belgrade: Savezni zavod za statistiku, 1954); Statistički Godišnjak Jugoslavije (Knj. 35) (Belgrade: Savezni zavod za statistiku, 1988).

force on people the kind of choices that have led to the current conflict.[50] Moreover, the composition of the census form, which required respondents to declare a single mother tongue, effectively erased the multilingualism that has characterized the Balkans for centuries—if not millennia—and that is still a significant feature of Macedonian life in some areas.[51]

Lability of identity has long been a feature of life in Macedonia. The oldest generation from Western Macedonia remembers when Christians and Muslims would live under the same roof as part of the same extended family. Before the Mürszteg agreement of October 2–3, 1903, only Muslims could serve as gendarmes, and such officials had significant power at the local level.[52] In Christian families, therefore, it was not uncommon for one brother to convert to Islam in order to be in a position to protect the entire family. Everyone ate at a common table, and if, for example, pork were available and a *zelnik* (pie) was made, the women of the house would put pork in only half the pita and both the Christian and Muslim sides of the family would eat from the same pan. Marriages have always been freely contracted along religious lines but across linguistic ones. The children of such "mixed" marriages would grow up bilingual or multilingual. In recent times, when faced with the necessity of choosing a nationality, choices can follow gender lines; for example, if a Turkish man marries an Albanian woman, the sons may be Turks and the daughters Albanian, while in other families the choice may be for one son to be Albanian and one to be Turkish. The European concept of nationality, equating ethnicity with language with state, does not correspond to the complex realities of Macedonia (nor of many, perhaps most, other countries), and by focusing on "nationality" to the exclusion of other characteristics we get contradictory situations such as those of parents insisting that their children be schooled in a language that they do not know despite the fact that the primary justification for multilingual education at the elementary level is that children learn best when taught in their mother tongue.[53]

The politicization of the language issue and its confusion with nationality in the 1994 census was highlighted in several incidents that occurred in Albanian-speaking villages in southwestern Macedonia, where citizens objected because some of the Albanian-speaking enumerators were not ethnic Albanians but rather Roms (Gypsies), Ǵupci ("Egyptians"), or Vlahs.[54] Since most Ǵupci in southwestern Macedonia have Albanian as their first language, and many Roms and Vlahs are fluent in it—especially in southwestern Macedonia—the issue clearly was not a question of the right to register in one's mother tongue, but rather a demand for an ethnic Albanian, that is, an instance of ethnic prejudice.

The events leading up to the boycott of the 1991 census, the impo-sition of the 1994 census, and subsequent developments show a pat-tern of manipulation and fragmentation of ethnic and linguistic identities utilizing legitimate grievances to benefit certain types of polit-ical elites. At the time of the census, my assessment was that it would prove a statistical success but a political failure. Insofar as it has not resulted in any significant changes in the figures—both official and purported—according to which ethnically based political relations are determined, this prediction has held true. The ICOM final report, while not uncritical, affirmed that the census was carried out according to "European" or "international" standards. It has been refuted by the Albanian political actors who brought it about, but at the same time they have generally continued to try to work within the existing gov-ernmental framework. In January 1995, the constitutional court ruled that article 35 of the census law, which governed language use, was unconstitutional, that is, contrary to article 7, which declares Macedonian the official language and guarantees (or restricts) official minority language use at (or to) the local level.[55] Thus the census law solved nothing in this respect, and when I returned to Macedonia in December 1995 as part of the fact-finding mission for the South Balkans Working Group of the Center for Preventive Action, the question of language use at the federal level was still the focus of significant polit-ical tension.

AFTER THE CENSUS IS OVER

If one of the purposes of the externally sponsored census was either to legitimize or to silence Albanian claims and thereby promote in one way or another greater stability in Macedonian society, the presence of European mediators in the ongoing dispute is not necessarily serving to promote stabilization. In an editorial published by the outspoken, albeit government-dependent, weekly *Puls* more than half a year after the census ended, Ambassador Ahrens is cited in the following terms:

> Arens [sic] developed a thesis of a parallel existence instead of a common existence between ethnic groups in Macedonia, particularly between Macedonians and ethnic Albanians. According to Arens, "there never was a true coexistence," but nationalities in Macedonia "have always led parallel lives." He said he had the feeling that he probably knows

more about Albanian history and culture than the average Macedonian. Also, he had the impression that nationalities had aversions to one other. He backed this claim by the fact that there are no mixed marriages, and there are ethnic tensions in both public and private communication, especially between Macedonians and Albanians.[56]

This is a significant departure from Dr. Ahrens' admonishment to Albanian politicians at the beginning of the census, when they were still threatening a boycott. At that time, he told them they were in the same boat with the Macedonians, and that if they—the Albanians—rocked the boat, they would all drown. My own experience with journalists has sensitized me to the fact that what appears in the press is not always what was actually said, but regardless of its accuracy, the statement itself is an exemplary instance of a present construction being projected onto the past. It imposes a view of Macedonian reality that at the same time serves the interest of the local political elite that gives a diplomat his international legitimacy and promotes a version of the history of Macedonia that is at variance with concrete evidence—for example, the assistant minister of education is the son of an Albanian father and a Macedonian mother, the prime minister's brother-in-law is a Turk, a Macedonian friend of mine who used to work in the government has an Albanian wife—but also helps to reify modern ethnic conflicts.

In a slightly broader context, Todorova[57] also projects the present onto the past, albeit for quite different reasons, when she attempts to define the term "Balkanism" only as "politically and ethnically fragmented" or, citing Bercovici, "Austro-Hungarian political policy relating to the Balkans."[58] There is, however, a widely accepted meaning of the term "Balkanism" that is precisely the opposite of fragmented. In linguistics, a Balkanism is a feature shared among the unrelated or only distantly related languages of the Balkans. The grammatical structures of the Balkan languages attest to centuries of multilingualism and interethnic contact at the most intimate levels. Some features shared by Balkan Slavic, Balkan Romance, Albanian, Greek, and even some Balkan Turkish dialects result from people speaking each others' languages.[59] During the 1994 census, Debar proved to be the most intractable commune (for reasons relating more to competition between the periphery and the center than between ethnicities), and in the end it was the only commune in which the census was not completed. And yet, the Albanian and Macedonian dialects of Debar provide a striking example of phonological similarity that results from centuries of bilingualism.

The Organization for Security and Cooperation in Europe (OSCE) mission that was stationed in Skopje in December 1995 provided other examples of the need for outside observers to be better informed. I encountered among members of the mission the misconception that Macedonian is a "really a Bulgarian dialect," an attitude that displays a remarkable insensitivity to the milieu in which they were supposed to operate as mediators.[60] I was particularly curious about an incident that had occurred in the village of Ognjanci. At the time of the census, I made the following observation concerning that village in my notes: "A mixed village (Macedonians, Turks, Albanians, Roms). It was reported that interethnic relations are excellent and everyone cooperated happily with the census."[61] And yet a little more than a year later the following news item appeared:

> Yesterday in the Skopje village Ognjanci, a group of citizens of Macedonian and Serbian nationality tried to prevent the entrance in the school to 40 children of Albanian nationality. There was no incident because the police without using force dispersed the gathered people. The Ministry for Education has decided to include the teaching on the Albanian language for the Albanian children in the same school. Those protesting think that the school was built by them, and will not allow their children to learn in combined classes with children from different grades. They offer a solution—the children of Albanian nationality to continue their education in the former barrack in the village, until the Ministry reconsiders its own decision and finally decides who the school building will be given to. Minister of Education, Emilija Simoska, for the Macedonian TV stated the Ministry does not intend to succumb to any kind of formal pressure and unless there is some disturbances among local people, assistance from Ministry of Interior will be asked. [sic][62]

The OSCE had involved itself in the affair, which had been resolved peacefully. But when I inquired of one of the mission's members how it was that interethnic relations had deteriorated so significantly in so short a time, my informant responded: "Maybe they were Serbs. We never found out. All we care about is human rights, and then we move on."

This same member of the OSCE mission told me of their experience in Debarska Župa, where Macedonian-speaking Muslim parents have recently been demanding Turkish-language schools for their children (recall the incident in Bačište cited above). The OSCE observer informed me that they had met the Turkish teacher who called on children "randomly" to demonstrate how well they spoke Turkish.[63] The observer also told me that the grandparents spoke Turkish, implying that the parents were seeking to return the children to their roots.[64] I asked the observer if they had spoken with any of the families. The observer responded that they did not visit any homes and did not care what the home language actually was. Parents have the human right to choose the language of the children's school even if the decision handicaps the children by requiring them to begin school in a language they do not know. The circumstances that lead to such a situation and the resolution of the deeper causes of the problems it represents were explicitly of no interest. As with the ICOM observers, so, too, the OSCE mission does not appear to be prepared to address the complexities of the specific context in which it finds itself.

STATISTICAL SUCCESS, POLITICAL FAILURE: "EUROPE," THE INTERNATIONAL COMMUNITY, AND THE FUTURE OF THE BALKANS

The 1994 census highlighted, among other things, the ambiguity of the term *Europe*. Geographically, it refers to a continent bounded by the Mediterranean and Black Seas, the southern slopes of the Caucasus and the western slopes of the Urals. Politically or culturally, however, the term "Europe" often still has the meaning of "Western Europe" or "Europe of the Great Powers." Thus, for example, the most powerful political unit on the continent calls itself the European Union, although only Western European nations plus Greece are included in it. It is no coincidence that Greece has embarked on a vigorous internal propaganda campaign stressing its membership in this Europe. The exclusion of the southeastern peninsula of geographical Europe from what can be called political Europe is well known in the Balkans.[65] The sense of alienation generated thereby was eloquently expressed by the Bulgarian author and journalist Aleko Konstantinov at the end of a vignette in his famous work *Baj Ganjo*, which satirizes the adventures of a Bulgarian rose-oil merchant in the Western Europe of his day and subsequently in then newly liberated Bulgaria.[66] In the penultimate sentence of the story *Baj Ganjo žurnalist* ("Baj Ganjo as a Journalist"), Konstantinov writes, "*Evropejci sme nij, ama vse ne sme dotam!*" ("We're Europeans—but still not quite!") I heard a comparable use of the term "Europe" during the 1994 census, when an ethnic Albanian politician brought me with him into a restricted building, explaining to the guard (in Macedonian): *"Toj e od Evropa"* ("He is from Europe"). My companion knew that I was an American and an employee of UNPRO-FOR, but he identified me as *od Evropa* because my role at that moment was that of a privileged Western outsider, just like a member of ICOM. Insofar as international European organizations succeeded in pressuring Macedonia into conducting a census that they funded and observed, it can be argued that political Europe was exerting authority in geographical Europe's southeastern periphery and particularly in Macedonia as a periphery of peripheries.[67]

This Europe was utilized by both Albanian and Macedonian political actors to further their particular goals. The Albanian politicians mobilized quite legitimate social and political grievances based on very real discrimination against ethnic Albanian citizens of Macedonia, ranging from censorship and restriction of language and property rights to firings and jail sentences—especially since 1981—to further their own careers and demands for autonomy, federalization, and ultimately irredentism.[68] Macedonian statisticians and politicians were faced with a choice between an externally imposed census or further destabilization caused by a loss of legitimacy in an international community that was at that time permitting Macedonia's economic strangulation while continuing to prevent the full realization of its sovereignty; they chose the census. But they then imposed their own condition, namely that the funding be sufficient to cover not merely the nationality question, which was the only one Europe sought to resolve and the only one that Albanian ethnopoliticians could use to legitimize their claims on the international scene, but also all those features of the Macedonian economy (such as agricultural property and land use) that form part of a complete census but that had been omitted from the 1991 census because of insufficient funding resulting from the economic crisis.

The 1994 census was in sum a statistical success but a political failure. Although it legitimated the basic statistics of the 1991 census, it did nothing to resolve the issues of political hegemony and access to resources that continue to plague Macedonia. It did, however, help to reify a conflict whose roots in Macedonian history are not as deep as some political actors would pretend. In seeking to impose a vision of nationality that does not correspond to Macedonia's complex cultural context, political Europe reproduced its vision of Balkan "otherness" and marginality in Macedonia more than it contributed to its stabilization.

The continued presence of various international organizations and actors in Macedonia and the ongoing tensions in the region raise the question of how the current Balkan crisis can best be resolved. Hayden in his review of Woodward makes the point that scholars specializing in southeastern Europe—one can add many of them trained with the help of U.S. federal education grants designated specifically for the creation of a cadre of area specialists—were not consulted when U.S. government policies concerning the former Yugoslavia were discussed and adopted.[69] The activities of international organizations illustrated in the foregoing exposition reveal a similar exclusion of regional expertise. If the future is to be different from the past, a closer cooperation between scholars and political actors is one way to promote the kind of understanding that could lead to stability.

THE SOUTH BALKANS
WORKING GROUP

MEMBERS OF THE WORKING GROUP

The members of the working group are listed below. Those marked with an asterisk (*) participated in the December mission to the region.

SEYMOUR TOPPING* is the chair of the working group. He is the administrator of the Pulitzer Prizes and the Sanpaolo Professor of international journalism at Columbia University's Graduate School of Journalism. Topping has had a distinguished career at the *New York Times* where he was a correspondent, foreign editor, and managing editor.

PAULA J. DOBRIANSKY is senior international affairs and trade advisor at the law firm of Hunton & Williams. In this capacity Dr. Dobriansky advises the firm and its clients on political, economic, and trade trends in Central and Eastern Europe and the former Soviet Union. She is also the host of *Freedom's Challenge* on National Empowerment Television and an adjunct fellow at the Hudson Institute. She has previously served in the State Department, U.S. Information Agency, and the National Security Council.

VICTOR A. FRIEDMAN* is a professor of Slavic and Balkan linguistics at the University of Chicago. He is a widely recognized expert on Macedonia and Albania and has published extensively in the field. Friedman has served in Macedonia as an advisor to the United Nations Protection Forces and is fluent in Macedonian and Albanian.

HURST HANNUM is academic dean and associate professor of international law at the Fletcher School of Law and Diplomacy at Tufts University. A specialist on questions of self-determination, autonomy, and human rights, Hannum was director of the Procedural Aspects of International Law Institute, a fellow at the United States Institute of Peace, and has served as counsel in cases before the European and Inter-American Commissions on Human Rights and the United Nations.

JANE E. HOLL is the executive director of the Carnegie Commission on Preventing Deadly Conflict. Before joining the Carnegie Commission, Holl was a career officer in the U.S. Army and served most recently as director for European Affairs on the National Security Council.

JERI LABER is currently senior advisor to Human Rights Watch. Until 1995 she was executive director of Human Rights Watch/Helsinki, formerly known as Helsinki Watch. Laber also serves as executive director of the International Freedom to Publish Committee of the Association of American Publishers.

F. STEPHEN LARRABEE* is a senior staff member in the International Policy Department at RAND. Before joining RAND he served as vice president and director of studies at the Institute of East-West Security Studies and was also a scholar in residence at the Institute. Larrabee has served on the U.S. National Security Council staff, has taught at several universities, and has written numerous books.

HERBERT S. OKUN is executive director of the Financial Services Volunteer Corps. Okun served in the U.S. Foreign Service from 1955 to 1991 and was most recently special advisor on Yugoslavia and deputy to former secretary of state Cyrus Vance in the latter's capacity as UN mediator between Greece and Macedonia. He has been U.S. deputy permanent representative and ambassador to the United Nations and was the U.S. ambassador to the German Democratic Republic.

EDITH B. PAGE is manager of infrastructure and transportation for the Bechtel Corporation. She works closely with United Infrastructure Company, Bechtel's joint venture with Kiewit Company for public/private ventures in infrastructure. Page is currently involved in studies of an East-West transport corridor in the South Balkans.

ROY WILLIAMS* is vice president and director of overseas programs at the International Rescue Committee. Williams has long been involved with refugee work and has extensive experience in humanitarian issues in the former Yugoslavia.

CONSULTANTS TO THE WORKING GROUP

Three specialists acted as consultants to the working group: Janie Leatherman prepared a paper for the group entitled "Untying Macedonia's Gordian Knot: Preventive Diplomacy in the Southern Balkans"; David L. Phillips organized the mission, provided key technical assistance, and undertook background research in international policy; and Steven L. Burg prepared a background paper for the group and wrote much of the report that appears in this volume.

STEVEN L. BURG* is a professor in the Department of Politics at Brandeis University and the principal consultant for the group. He is a specialist on the former Yugoslavia.

JANIE LEATHERMAN* is a visiting research professor at the Kroc Institute for International Peace Studies at the University of Notre Dame. She is an expert on international mediation and conflict prevention.

DAVID L. PHILLIPS* is director of the European Centre for Common Ground and senior research associate at the International Peace Research Institute, Oslo.

CENTER FOR PREVENTIVE ACTION STAFF

BARNETT R. RUBIN* is the director of the Center for Preventive Action at the Council on Foreign Relations. Previously, he was associate professor of political science and director of the Project on Political

Order and Conflict in the Former Soviet Union at Columbia University. He has also taught at Yale University and was a fellow of the U.S. Institute of Peace.

ANYA SCHMEMANN is a program associate with the Center for Preventive Action. She received her B.A. from Harvard-Radcliffe College and her M.A. from the Russian Research Center at Harvard University.

THE ADVISORY BOARD OF THE CENTER FOR PREVENTIVE ACTION

Chair:
JOHN W. VESSEY
(ret.) Chairman, Joint Chiefs of Staff

Vice Chairs:
FRANCES FITZGERALD
The New Yorker

SAMUEL LEWIS
(ret.) U.S. Institute of Peace and
U.S. Department of State

Board:

MORTON ABRAMOWITZ
Carnegie Endowment for International Peace

GRAHAM ALLISON
Harvard University

CRAIG ANDERSON
General Theological Seminary

JAMES E. BAKER
(ret.) UN and U.S. Department
of State

DENIS A. BOVIN
Bear Stearns & Co.

ANTONIA HANDLER CHAYES
Conflict Management Group

VIVIAN LOWERY DERRYCK
Africa Leadership Forum

ROBERT P. DEVECCHI
International Rescue Committee

PETER W. ECCLES
Eccles Associates

LESLIE H. GELB (ex officio)
Council on Foreign Relations

LOUIS GERBER
Communications Workers of America

ANDREW J. GOODPASTER
Atlantic Council

ERNEST G. GREEN
Lehman Brothers

SIDNEY HARMAN
Harman International Industries

JAMES W. HARPEL
Harpel Partners, L.P.

ARTHUR HERTZBERG

JANE E. HOLL
Carnegie Commission on
Preventing Deadly Conflict

SCOTT HORTON
Patterson, Belknap, Webb & Tyler

HENRY KAUFMAN
Henry Kaufman Associates

RICHARD C. LEONE
Twentieth Century Fund, Inc.

WENDY W. LUERS
The Foundation for a Civil Society

MICHAEL LUND
Creative Associates International, Inc.

ERNEST MAY
Harvard University

JAY MAZUR
Union of Needle Trades, Industrial
and Textile Employees

GAY MCDOUGALL
International Human Rights Law
Group

DONALD MCHENRY
Georgetown University

JOSEPH A. O'HARE
Fordham University

PEARL ROBINSON
Tufts University

LIONEL ROSENBLATT
Refugees International

KENNETH ROTH
Human Rights Watch

BARNETT R. RUBIN (ex officio)
CPA, Council on Foreign
Relations

KURT SCHMOKE
Mayor of Baltimore

DONALD SHRIVER
Union Theological Seminary

HEDRICK SMITH
Johns Hopkins University

JOHN STEINBRUNER
Brookings Institution

FRITZ STERN
Columbia University

JULIA TAFT
InterAction

SEYMOUR TOPPING
Columbia School of Journalism

HARRY TRAIN
Strategic Research and
Management Services

BERNARD TRAINOR
Harvard University

ROBERT WAGGONER
Burrelle's Information Services

MICHAELA WALSH
Women's World Banking

ROY WILLIAMS
International Rescue Committee

R. JAMES WOOLSEY
Shea & Gardner

ARISTIDE ZOLBERG
New School for Social Research

NOTES

— 1 —

1. This section was written by Barnett R. Rubin with helpful comments from Steven L. Burg, David L. Phillips, Lori Fisler Damrosch, and an anonymous reviewer.

2. In this report we use the internationally accepted "Kosovo" rather than the Albanian "Kosova," except when referring to institutions whose names use the latter spelling. We refer to the Republic of Macedonia as such (or as "Macedonia"), while recognizing that the adjacent region of northern Greece has the same name. We do not use the term "Former Yugoslav Republic of Macedonia" (FYROM), which is still employed by some countries and international organizations.

3. Yugoslavia originated as the Kingdom of the Serbs, Croats, and Slovenes. Tito's original Yugoslav constitution listed Serbs, Croats, Slovenes, Montenegrins, and Macedonians as constituent nations. The 1974 constitution added Muslims. Muslim ethnic Albanians generally declared themselves as Albanians rather than Muslims.

4. The "outer wall of sanctions" generally refers to full diplomatic recognition of the FRY; the FRY's full, active membership in international organizations, mainly the UN and OSCE; its membership in international financial institutions (the World Bank, the European Bank for Reconstruction and Development, and the International Monetary Fund); and the release to the FRY of contested assets. Official U.S. policy states that breaches in the "outer wall" will depend on normalization of relations among the five successor states of the Socialist Federal Republic of Yugoslavia, restoration of political and human rights in Kosovo, fulfillment of obligations under the Dayton accords, and cooperation with the International War Crimes Tribunal.

— **2** —

1. This chapter was written by Steven L. Burg and Barnett R. Rubin.

2. This is the argument contained in an official publication distributed to the delegation during our meetings in Belgrade entitled *Kosovo and Metohija: An integral part of the Republic of Serbia and FR of Yugoslavia—Documents and Facts* (Belgrade, 1995).

3. *Reuters* (Belgrade, February 5, 1996), electronic mail edition.

4. Open Media Research Institute (OMRI), *Daily Digest* 35, II (February 19, 1996), electronic mail edition.

5. *Associated Press* (Tirana, December 26, 1995).

6. As president of parliament, Andov served as the Council's chair until his resignation in February 1996.

— **3** —

1. *New York Times*, December 28, 1992.

. 2. Quotations in these chapters denote extracts from field notes. These should be treated as close paraphrasing of an actual statement. Except where the discussions are noted as having been conducted in English, these are also translations (originals in Serbian, Macedonian, or Albanian).

3. "Kosovo" is the Serbo-Croatian form and the current legal name of the region. "Kosova" is the Albanian form and the preferred usage of the Democratic League of Kosova (LDK).The former will be used here to refer to the region, except when referring to the LDK or its government.

4. Peter R. Prifti, *Kosovo in Ferment*, Report C/69–15 (Cambridge, MA: MIT Center for International Studies, June 1969).

5. The ethnic Albanian argument for the distinct—and Albanian—identity of Kosovo is presented in Rexhep Ismajli, *Kosova and the Albanians in Former Yugoslavia* (Prishtina: Kosova Information Center, n.d.).

6. Savezni Zavod za Statistiku (SZS), *Statisticki bilten 1295* "Nacionalni sastav stanovnistva po opstinama" ("National composition of the population by counties") (Belgrade, 1982), p. 16.

7. SZS, *Statisticki bilten 1934* "Nacionalni sastav stanovnistva po opstinama" ("National composition of the population by counties") (Belgrade, 1992), p. 42.

8. Ismajli, *Kosova and the Albanians*, p. 64.

9. "Kosovar" is the term used in both Serbian and Albanian to refer to the ethnic Albanian population of Kosovo.

10. Stefan Troebst, "Macedonia: Powder Keg Defused?" *RFE/RL Research Report* 3, no 4 (January 28, 1994), p. 36.

11. Fabian Schmidt, "From National Consensus to Pluralism," *Transition* (March 29, 1995), p. 26.

12. Elez Biberaj, *Kosova: The Balkan Powder Keg,* Conflict Studies 258 (London: Research Institute for the Study of Conflict and Terrorism, February 1993), pp. 12–13.

13. Steven L. Burg, "New Data on the League of Communists of Yugoslavia," *Slavic Review* 46, no. 3/4 (Fall/Winter 1987), table 7, p. 558.

14. Constitution (1974) of the Socialist Republic of Macedonia, as cited in Borislav T. Blagojevic, ed., *Uporedni Pregled Republickih i Pokrajinskih Ustava 1974,* (Comparative Review of the Republic and Provincial Constitutions of 1974) (Belgrade: Institut za Uporedno Pravo [Institute of Comparative Law], 1974), pp. 15, 17, 32.

15. *Constitution of the Republic of Macedonia* (Skopje, 1991), preamble.

16. Hugh Poulton, "The Republic of Macedonia after UN Recognition," *RFE/RL Research Report* 2, no. 23 (June 4, 1993), p. 23.

17. Duncan M. Perry, "On the Road to Stability—or Destruction?" *Transition* (August 25, 1995), p. 46.

18. Poulton, "The Republic of Macedonia after UN Recognition," p. 22. The full name of the opposition party is Internal Macedonian Revolutionary Organization-Democratic Party for Macedonian National Unity, or VMRO-DPMNE in its Macedonian acronym.

19. Robert Austin, "Albanian-Macedonian Relations: Confrontation or Cooperation?" *RFE/RL Research Report* 2, no. 42 (October 22, 1993), p. 24.

20. UN Security Council document S/RES/795 (December 11, 1992).

21. The Organization for Security and Cooperation in Europe (OSCE) was known as the Conference on Security and Cooperation in Europe (CSCE) until January 1995. To avoid confusion we have used the term OSCE, even when it is an anachronism.

22. UN Security Council document S/1995/222 (March 22, 1995), p. 14.

23. UN Security Council document S/1996/65 (January 30, 1996).

24. *Macedonia Information and Liaison Service (MILS) News,* Skopje (April 9, 1996), electronic mail edition.

25. CSCE Communication no. 305, "HCNM recommendations concerning inter-ethnic relations in FYR of Macedonia" (Prague, November 24, 1993).

26. Office of Democratic Institutions and Human Rights *ODIHR Bulletin* 3, no. 2 (Spring 1995), pp. 56–57.

27. For the high commissioner's own statement of this approach, see OSCE, *ODIHR Bulletin* 3, no. 3 (Fall 1995), pp. 40–45.

28. Carl Bildt is the international community's High Representative in charge of the civilian implementation of the Dayton agreement.

29. Poulton, "The Republic of Macedonia after UN Recognition," p. 25.

30. See Victor A. Friedman's chapter in this volume, pp. 89–91.

31. Republicki zavod za statistika, *Soopstenie 1* "Popis '94: Podatoci za segasnosta i idninata, prvi rezultati" ("Census '94: Data for the present and the future, first results") (Skopje, 1994), p. 28.

32. See Friedman's chapter in this volume, p. 89.

33. Ibid, pp. 89, 92–95.

━ 4 ━

1. Nina Dobrkovic, "Juzni Tirol—model za resavanje polozaja i statusa nacionalnih manjina?" ("South Tyrol—model for resolution of the position and status of national minorities?") *Medjunarodni Problemi* 44, no. 3–4 (1992), pp. 272–86.

2. F. Gunther Eyck, "South Tyrol and Multiethnic Relations," in Joseph V. Montville, ed., *Conflict and Peacemaking in Multiethnic Societies* (Lexington, MA: Lexington Books, 1990), pp. 219–38.

3. Momcilo Petrovic, *Pitao Sam Albance Sta Zele a Oni Su Rekli: Republiku . . . Ako Može* ("I Asked Albanians What They Want and They Answered: A Republic . . . If Possible") (Belgrade: Radio B92, 1996).

4. Democratic Center, *News Release* 1, no. 2–3 (September 1995), and Project on Ethnic Relations, *Domestic Processes and Ethnic Relations in Yugoslavia* (Princeton: 1995).

5. Two sources represent authoritative interpretations of the constitutional order established in 1974. One is the 1975 edition of the text on constitutional law by Yugoslavia's long-time leading expert, Jovan Djordjevic, *Ustavno Pravo* (Belgrade: Savremena Administracija, 1975). The other is a volume of article-by-article explanation and commentary prepared by a group of 15 authors, eight of whom participated directly in drafting the constitution itself: *Ustav Socijalisticke Federativne Republike Jugoslavije: Strucno objasnjenje* (Belgrade: Privredni Pregled, 1975). These texts make clear the formal subordination of the provinces to Serbia. For an examination of the status of the provinces vis-a-vis the republics in federal decisionmaking processes, see Steven L. Burg, *Conflict and Cohesion in Socialist Yugoslavia: Political Decision Making Since 1966* (Princeton: Princeton University Press, 1983).

6. Strong statements of the various dimensions of the Kosovar claim are to be found in a publication distributed to the delegation by the LDK during our visit; see Gazmend Zajmi, *Dimensions of the Question of Kosova in the Balkans* (Prishtina, 1994).

7. The governing coalition in Macedonia and the composition of the council of ministers, has changed since the delegation's visit. This report refers to individual ministers serving at the time of our visit, in December 1995.

8. The minister's translator rendered the Macedonian "neguva" as "cherish," in which case this statement would read "cherish the culture." In the context of the minister's remarks, however, "neguva" is more accurately translated as "preserve."

9. July 1995 draft, provided to the delegation by the ministry.

10. "Mak-News" electronic mail edition (February 12, 1996). The PPD posts include the ministers of the economy, economic development, labor and social policy, science, and one minister without portfolio.

11. See Petrovic, *Pitao Sam Albance,* for examples of differing attitudes toward this option.

— Appendix A —

1. This section was written by Victor A. Friedman and represents his views solely.

Author's note: This paper is an expanded and updated version of an earlier work that appeared as Woodrow Wilson Center Occasional Paper 44 under the title "Populations and Powder Kegs: The Macedonian Census of 1994 in Historical Perspective." I wish to thank Dr. John Lampe of the Woodrow Wilson Center for his helpful comments on that version of the paper. I am grateful to Dr. Svetlana Antonovska, director of the Bureau of Statistics of the Republic of Macedonia, who has been unfailingly generous with her time and with documentation. I also wish to thank Ms. Jela Markovska of the same bureau, who kindly expedited my certification as a census observer. To all the other workers at the bureau of statistics as well as to Risto Ivanov, head of the census commission, my sincere thanks for their time and efforts. I owe a special debt of gratitude to Janusz Sznajder, deputy chief of civil affairs at United Nations Protection Forces headquarters in Skopje, who was unfailingly supportive of my mission at UNPROFOR (the Macedonian branch of which is now UNPREDEP) and who was instrumental in my contacting key actors in the 1994 Macedonian census. To the local staff and to the military side of UNPROFOR, as well as to Mark Penn, Elizabeth Baldwin, Tiki Salvado, Sandra Marchesa, Angel, Sasho, Sanya, Sonya, and Tina on the civil affairs side, my sincere thanks for their support. I am extraordinarily grateful to Dr. Susan Woodward of the Brookings Institution, who, as head of the Analysis and Assessment Unit for the Office of the Special Representative of the Secretary General, attached to UNPROFOR in former Yugoslavia, invited me to join her team during the summer of 1994 as a senior policy and political analyst. Without her invitation this paper could never have been written. Both she and Prof. Susan Gal of the University of Chicago as well as Dr. Janie Leatherman of the University of Notre Dame read earlier versions of this paper, and I am grateful for their comments and encouragement. I am similarly grateful to Prof. Steven L. Burg of Brandeis University for his helpful comments on the present version of the paper. I also wish to thank those members of the International Commission on Former Yugoslavia, the International Census Observation Mission, and the Group of Experts who kindly permitted me to attend some of their meetings in my capacity as an analyst for UNPROFOR. I am also grateful to the many Macedonian and Albanian politicians and activists who kindly consented to meet with me, as well as to the many other citizens of the Republic of Macedonia of all nationalities who showed me unfailing courtesy and warm hospitality. I wish to express a special debt of gratitude to the Ministry for Information of the Republic of Macedonia, which for more than twenty years has supported my research by supplying me with newspapers, magazines, journals, and books. Research for this publication was supported in part by a grant from the International Researches and Exchanges

Board, with funds provided by the National Endowment for the Humanities, which enabled me to return to Skopje in May 1995. Additional material was gathered when I was a member of the December 1995 fact-finding mission of the South Balkans Working Group of the Center for Preventive Action of the Council on Foreign Relations. None of these organizations or individuals is responsible for the views expressed. The opinions and analyses expressed in this article are entirely my own and do not represent those of any of the organizations and individuals named or mentioned above. Any responsibility for error is mine.

2. For an example of a Great Power view of the causes of World War I that bears striking resemblance to some modern attempts to lay the entire blame for the collapse of Yugoslavia at a single doorstep, see Edith Durham, *The Serajevo Crime* (London: George Allen & Unwin, 1925). See also Maria Todorova, "The Balkans: From Discovery to Invention," *Slavic Review* 53 (1994), p. 460, on recent attempts to resuscitate the myth of Balkan responsibility for World War I.

3. Throughout this paper, the term "Macedonia" will be used in both its geographical and political senses depending on the relevant time period. For the time period up to the Treaty of Bucharest in 1913, "Macedonia" refers to the geographic region defined by Mount Olympus, the Pindus range, Mount Šar, Mount Rila, the western Rhodopes, and the river Mesta (Greek Nestos). After 1913, unmodified "Macedonia" refers to the part of geographic Macedonia that was given to Serbia by the Treaty of Bucharest and that, with a few border adjustments resulting from subsequent treaties and administrative acts, ultimately became the Republic of Macedonia in 1991. Other parts of geographic Macedonia for the period after 1913 are referred to with additional modifiers, such as Greek (Aegean) Macedonia, Bulgarian (Pirin) Macedonia, Golo Brdo and Lower Prespa (Albanian Macedonia).

4. Although the veracity of the 1989 Albanian census figures on minorities has been questioned—the census officially registered about 5,000 Macedonians, for example, while sources in Macedonia insisted the number is twenty to thirty times greater (*Nova Makedonija*, February 2, 1990)—it is generally acknowledged that Albanians constitute the majority in Albania.

5. For an objective and scholarly discussion of the linguistic issues by an American expert in Slavic linguistics, see Horace Lunt, "Some Sociolinguistic Aspects of Macedonian and Bulgarian," in B. Stolz, I. Titunik, and L. Doležel, eds., *Language and Literary Theory: In Honor of Ladislav Matejka* (Ann Arbor: University of Michigan, 1984), pp. 83–132; Robert D. Kaplan, "History's Cauldron," *The Atlantic Monthly* (June 1991), p.103; Hugh Poulton, *Who Are the Macedonians?* (Bloomington: Indiana University Press, 1995), p. 116; and Misha Glenny, "The Birth of a Nation" (review of Poulton), *The New York Review of Books* (November 16, 1995), p. 24 all fail to grasp the significance of this type of equivocation. Thus, for example, Poulton on page 116 privileges Bulgarian attempts to claim Macedonian as a dialect of Bulgarian by uncritically citing as a "comprehensive refutation" of Macedonian "as a language

distinct from Bulgarian" a Bulgarian work first published as an article in the first number of the journal *Bălgarski ezik* in 1978. Lunt characterizes that work as "incompetent in terms of linguistic theory, and resting on a poorly organized series of propositions and claims, many of them dubious, exaggerated or false," pp. 87–88. Lunt notes that, "aside from a dignified answer by Macedonian linguists (see Todor Dimitrovski et al., *Za makedonskiot jazik* [Skopje: Institut za makedonski jazik, 1978]) this embarrassing aberration from common sense and sound scholarship aroused little response in print" (p. 88). Unfortunately, Poulton fails to cite that response. Similarly, Glenny writes: "Primarily, Bulgarian has a definite article and no case declension (unlike all other Slav languages until the Macedonians codified their Bulgarian dialect into a new language)" (p. 24). Aside from the facts that the sharing of two grammatical features is hardly justification for classifying one language as a dialect of another and that these two particular features are shared with the southern Serbian dialects, describing Macedonian as a Bulgarian dialect is like describing Norwegian as a Danish dialect. See Einar Haugen, "The Scandinavian Languages as Cultural Artifacts," in Joshua Fishman, Charles Ferguson, and J. Das Gupta, eds., *Language Problems of Developing Nations* (New York: John Wiley & Sons, 1968). See also Horace Lunt, "On Macedonian Language and Nationalism," *Slavic Review* 45, no. 4 (1986), pp. 729–34.

6. Henry Alford, *Alford's Greek Testament: An Exigetical and Critical Commentary*, vol. 1 (Grand Rapids, MI: Baker, 1980; first published in 1874), pp. 456–57.

7. Although U.S. officials reportedly supported the extraordinary census in their private discussions with Macedonian leaders, there was no public U.S. support or participation. The census was essentially a "European" event taking place on Macedonian territory.

8. Christo A. Dako, *Albania: The Master Key to the Near East* (Boston: Grimes, 1919), p. 75.

9. It is significant that, while claiming factors other than language as the determiners of nationality, every Greek government has prohibited education in the languages of Greek Orthodox Christians other than Greek. That is because language can function as the determiner of nationality or as a pathway to altered ethnic self-identification, although it does not always do so. It is likewise significant that the Greek-speaking minority of Albania is never referred to as "hellenophone Albanians."

10. Compare Osman Yavuz Saral, *Kaybettiğmiz Rumeli* (Istanbul: Boğazici, 1975).

11. Similarities in folklore and folk traditions were also adduced to support Serbian claims.

12. Aleksandar Belić, *La Macédoine* (Paris: Bloud & Gay, 1919), p. 250.

13. Ibid., pp. 253–56, 264.

14. A. Vaillant, "Le Problème du Slave Macédonien," *Bulletin de la Société Linguistique de Paris* 39, no. 2 (1938), p. 119.

15. Vaillant mentions, for instance, the fate of the jers (short ĭ and ŭ) and juses (nasal ę and ǫ), /vŭ/, and vocalic /l/ and notes that vestiges of /št/ in the

/k/ area show that the latter reflex is the result of substitution; for example, in Galičnik gaki are "britches," but gašnik (in Bulgarian, gaštnik) is "a belt for holding up gaki," pp. 195–210.

16. Vaillant, "Le Problème du Slave Macédonien," pp. 304–8.

17. See Glenny, "The Birth of a Nation," p. 24, for an uncritical repetition of this type of linguistic claim with respect to Macedonian.

18. Vasil Kănčev, *Makedonija: Etnografija i Statistika* (Sofia: Bălgarsko Knižovno Družestvo, 1900), pp. 136–37.

19. Also absent here are Albanian and Romanian figures. Although Albanians laid claim to the western half of Macedonia as far as a line running from Kumanovo through Veles, the population figures that I have found in Albanian sources of the period do not attempt any ethnic breakdown but rather imply that the regions in question are simply Albanian with the occasional "colony" from some other ethnic group; see Dako, *Albania: The Master Key to the Near East*, p. 5. It would appear that the limits of Greater Albanian territorial claims were obtained by drawing a line connecting all the outlying Albanian-speaking villages of Epirus, Macedonia, Montenegro, and Serbia and then claiming all the territory inside those boundaries. In some respects, the Albanian situation at the turn of the century resembled the Macedonian: Albanian claims were marginalized because they lacked any Great Power support. Moreover, Turkey, which in this case functioned like other small powers such as Bulgaria, Greece, and Serbia, attempted to render the Albanians invisible by claiming them as Turks on the basis of religion (see Saral, *Kaybettiğimiz Rumeli*, p. 152). In this they would be supported by Greece, which claimed all of southern Albania on the basis of that part of the population that was Orthodox Christian. This left the Catholics of northern Albania, which Serbia and Montenegro were ready to absorb. Unlike the Macedonians, however, who, as Slavs speaking dialects midway between Serbian and Bulgarian, could be plausibly assimilated to one or the other even though they were arguably neither, the dialects of Albanian could not be linguistically claimed by any neighbors and were therefore instead discredited as being merely a *mischsprache*, a mixture of all the languages of the Balkans with almost no indigenous elements; see Gustav Meyer, *Etmologisches Wörterbuch der Albanesischen Sprache* (Strassburg: Trübner, 1891), p. ix. To this was added the claim that Albanians had no clearly defined national consciousness and that the north and south (*Geg* and *Tosk*) Albanian dialects were so different as to be incapable of uniting into a single language. On the first point, see P.N. Pipinelis, *Europe and the Albanian Question* (Chicago: Argonaut, 1963), p. 32; on the second, see A. Meillet, *Les Langues Dans L'Europe Nouvelle* (Paris: Payot, 1918), p. 255. Thus, aside from the use of religion as a means of denying legitimacy to both Macedonian and Albanian ethnic identity, both groups were also linguistically marginalized. Macedonians were told that they spoke either Bulgarian or Serbian, while Albanians were told that their language was not really a language at all. The Greeks had tried this type of strategy on the Bulgarians at an earlier period; see Cleanthes Nicolaïdes, *La Macédoine* (Berlin: Stuhr, 1899),

pp. 60, 120. The principal difference was that Albanians had sufficient national consciousness and political organization to lay claim successfully to a part of
the disintegrating Ottoman Empire in which they constituted a majority, while
the Macedonians were left completely out of these processes. Although the
Romanian government showed some interest in supporting Vlah claims, especially after the establishment of a Vlah Church (and therefore millet) in 1905,
the Romanians were too far away and the Vlahs too few in number and not
particularly strong in national consciousness. Those in the towns were mainly Greek-identified merchants while the transhumant shepherds of the coun-
tryside were hardly in a position to organize. Compare Keith Brown, *Of
Meanings and Memories: The National Imagination in Macedonia* (Ph.D. diss.,
University of Chicago, 1995).

20. See, for example, the map by Čupovski, in Ilija Petruševski, *Macedonia on
Old Maps* (Skopje: Detska Radost, 1992), p. 83, or Ǵorǵi Pulevski's statement
on Macedonian national consciousness in *Rečnik od Tri Jezika* (Belgrade:
Državna štamparija,1875), pp. 48–49. Also see Krste P. Misirkov's formula-
tion of Macedonian language and statehood in *Za Makedonckite Raboti* (Sofija:
Liberalnij Klub, 1903), p. 71; the correspondence concerning the Kostur
(Greek Kastoria) school of 1892, in Hristo Andonovski, "Makedonistiĉko
dviženje vo Kosturko," *Makedonija* 22, no. 387 (1985), p. 26; and Allen
Upward's account of his trip to Voden (Greek Edhessa) in *The East End of
Europe* (London: John Murray, 1908). Upward writes of an interview he conducted in a village two hours ride from Voden: "I asked what language they
spoke and my Greek interpreter carelessly rendered the answer 'Bulgare.' The
man himself had said 'Makedonski!' I drew attention to this word, and the
witness explained that he did not consider the rural dialect used in Macedonia
the same as Bulgarian, and refused to call it by that name. It was Macedonian,
a word to which he gave the Slave [sic] form of Makedonski." Upward continues: "The Exarchist claimed that his party had sixty or seventy houses in the
village; the Patriarchist had awarded him fifteen or twenty" (pp. 204–205).

21. Andrew Rossos, "The British Foreign Office and Macedonian National
Identity," *Slavic Review* 53, no. 369 (1994); see also his "Macedonianism and
Macedonian Nationalism on the Left," in Ivo Banac and Katherine Verdery,
eds., *National Character and National Ideology in Interwar Eastern Europe* (New
Haven: Yale Center for International and Area Studies, 1995), pp. 219–54.

22. Keith Brown, "Friction in the Archives: Nations and Negotiations on
Ellis Island, 1904" (Paper presented at the Tenth International Conference of
Europeanists, Chicago, March 1996).

23. See Kănčev, *Makedonija*, pp. 210–14, for figures from the end of the last
century.

24. Svetlana Antonovska and others, *Statistički Godišnik na Republika
Makedonija 1993* (Skopje: Republički Zavod za Statistika, 1994), p. 57.

25. A PPD campaign poster from the 1994 Macedonian elections gives symbolic representation to the PPD attempt to appeal to its Albanian constituency
and the European actors that have played such a significant role in supporting

its claims. The poster's slogan is in Albanian, English, and French. The poster thus erases both Macedonian and the other minority languages of Macedonia, while attempting to portray the party as oriented toward "Europe" (see the discussion of the term "Europe" at the end of this article).

26. Svetlana Antonovska and others, *Broj i Sruktura na Naselenieto vo Republika Makedonija po Opštini i Nacionalna Pripadnost: Sostojba 31.03.1991 Godina* (Skopje: Republički Zavod za Statistika, 1991).

27. Ibid.

28. The large variations in percentages are attributable not only to immigration and emigration, but also to sociopolitically motivated changes in choices in declaring identity. See Susan Gal, "Diversity and Contestation in Linguistic Ideologies: German Speakers in Hungary," *Language in Society* 22 (1993), pp. 337–59, and Darko Tanasković, "The Planning of Turkish as a Minority Language in Yugoslavia," in Ranko Bugarski and Celia Hawkesworth, eds., *Language Planning in Yugoslavia* (Columbus: Slavica, 1992), p. 143. The history and specifics of these phenomena are beyond the scope of this paper and deserve separate monographic treatment. My purpose in calling attention to them here is to emphasize that shifts in demography and shifts in identity are independent phenomena.

29. "Egyptians," in Macedonian "Ǵupci," "Eǵupci," or "Egipḱani" (also "Ǵuptin"), are descended from Roms but do not speak Romani and do not identify themselves as Roms. The ethnonyms themselves are cognate with English "Gypsy," which is derived from the claim or belief that the Romani people came from Egypt. The majority of Egipḱani live in Ohrid and Struga and speak Albanian, while those of Bitola speak Macedonian. Some Egipḱani attempted to register as a separate ethnic group in the 1981 census, but they were listed as "unknown" (*Sabota*, March 6, 1982). The Egipḱani claim to be descended from Egyptians, but there is no concrete evidence to support this claim. A more likely explanation is that they settled at a very early date and assimilated linguistically but not ethnically with non-Romani speakers and maintained ethnic separateness from Romani-speakers who were nomadic or became sedentarized at a later date. See Victor Friedman, "Problems in the Codification of a Standard Romani Literary Language," *Papers from the Fourth and Fifth Annual Meetings: Gypsy Lore Society, North American Chapter*, 1985, pp. 56–75; Ger Duijzings, "The Making of the Egyptians in Kosovo and Macedonia," in Hans Vermeulen and Cora Govers, eds., *The Politics of Ethnic Consciousness*, (Basingstoke: Macmillan, forthcoming); Ian Hancock, *A Handbook of Vlax Romani* (Columbus: Slavica, 1995), p. 17; Miodrag Hadži-Ristiḱ, "Prašanjeto na etnogenezata na Egipḱanite vo Makedonija," *Nova Makedonija*, September 13, 1994, p. 16; September 14, 1994, p. 16; September 15, 1994, p. 15; September 16, 1994, p. 22; September 17, 1994, p. 9; and Islam Abduramanoski, "Veštačka delba na Romite," *Nova Makedonija*, October 30, 1994, p. 7. The category "Bosniac" refers to Serbo-Croatian-speaking Muslims.

30. *Nova Makedonija,* April 20, 1991. Albanian-Americans repeated the same claim in an advertisement published on the *New York Times* op-ed page, March 27, 1996.

31. MILS, December 30, 1992, and Human Rights Watch/Helsinki Report, *The Macedonians of Greece* (New York: Human Rights Watch, 1994), p. 11.

32. MILS, January 13, 1993, and MILS, February 22, 1993.

33. MILS, November 25, 1992.

34. Niyazi Limanovski, head of the Association of Macedonian Muslims, came out against the census. Bekir Zhuta, a PPD minister in parliament and Albanian from Struga, stated that there was no need for help from outside. Radical Albanians accused both men of trying to divide and conquer, although Zhuta did serve as his party's spokesman in declaring the census invalid after the preliminary results were published; see MILS, April 13, 1994, and MILS, November 18, 1994.

35. Article 7 of the Macedonian constitution reads: "The Macedonian language, written using its Cyrillic alphabet, is the official language in the Republic of Macedonia. In the units of local self-government where the majority of the inhabitants belong to a nationality, in addition to the Macedonian language and Cyrillic alphabet, their language and alphabet are also in official use, in a manner determined by law. In the units of local self-government where there is a considerable number of inhabitants belonging to a nationality, their language and alphabet are also in official use, in addition to the Macedonian language and Cyrillic alphabet, under conditions and in a manner determined by law." The nationalities named are Albanians, Turks, Vlahs, and Roms, in that order. Serbs object to the fact that they are not specifically named but are subsumed under the expression "other nationalities." When the census law was being debated, Macedonian nationalists argued that the census forms should be only in Macedonian, since the census was being conducted at the national, not the local, level. In the end, however, bilingual forms were used for all five principal minority languages (but see the discussion later in this paper).

36. See Todorova, *The Balkans,* pp. 481–82.

37. The two exceptions were Greek historians from the Institute of Balkan Studies at Thessaloniki. According to information supplied to me by a member of the Group of Experts, there was originally one Greek appointed to the observation team, but the weekend before the team left for Macedonia, while the chief of the statistical bureau of the Council of Europe was away, the vice-chief, who was Greek, added another Greek to the team without the required approval of his superior. The Macedonian government granted both Greeks visas without demur. At the time Macedonia was under a Greek economic blockade, and holders of Macedonian passports could not enter Greece. Moreover, as indicated above, the official Greek position denies the existence of a Macedonian minority on its own territory (Human Rights Watch/Helsinki Report, *The Macedonians of Greece,* p. 11). The International Census Observation

Mission (ICOM) thus placed the Macedonian government in the position of granting privileges to citizens of a country that refused to do the same for Macedonians.

38. Arbër Xhaferi, "Regjistrimi i jashtëzakonshem i popullsisë," *Tribuna-Sh 2*, no. 23/24 (1994), pp. 20–21.

39. Significant lack of objectivity, however, was ascribed by Macedonian officials to a high-ranking member of the ICOM team who bore substantial responsibility for organizing the mission's work. She was perceived as being particularly difficult—even nasty. It is a measure of the tensions inherent in the situation that Macedonian officials speculated that this individual's peculiar behavior was because she was of Albanian descent, a rumor that I was unable to verify. The behavior of this individual that I observed myself led me to understand why Macedonian officials regarded her as a source, or at least an active supporter, of the adversarial attitude described later in this paper.

40. There are also two other Russian letters that do not occur in Macedonian.

41. In addition to the household forms filled out by the enumerators on the basis of answers given by those being interviewed, both enumerators and ICOM observers filled out supplementary, or "control," forms for the purposes of statistical verification and enumerating household members.

42. See Gal, "Diversity and Contestation in Linguistic Ideologies," p. 345, on abuses of the 1941 Hungarian census during the postwar period, when the 1941 census data, which was supposed to be confidential, was used to deport not only Germans in Hungary who had openly worked for the Nazis, but also anyone who had claimed German nationality and, later, anyone who had claimed German as their mother tongue. The 1994 Macedonian census was officially one of residents, not citizens.

43. There is a certain irony in the fact that some member countries of the European Union, such as Germany, have citizenship laws that are considerably more exclusionary than the Macedonian one.

44. That same day, June 22, 1995, an article appeared in *Nova Makedonija* asserting that international attention had exacerbated ethnic tension.

45. MILS, April 13, 1995. The polemic over figures also continued during the course of the census itself. An article in the Skopje-based Albanian-language daily newspaper *Flaka e vëllazërimit*, July 11, 1994, entitled "Over 8,000 Albanians," reported that one of the municipal instructors in Bitola claimed this figure for that municipality. "Any other figure connected with the number of Albanians given by the Bureau of Statistics will be declared a falsification. . . . I have so informed all communal, republic and international bodies" (my translation). This figure continued to be cited in the Albanian-language media even though the data had not yet been processed. The official preliminary figure for Albanians in the municipality of Bitola was 3,970. See Svetlana Antonovska and others, *Popis '94: Podatoci za segašnosta i idninata. Prvi rezultati. Soopštenie 1, Soopštenie 2* (Skopje: Republicki Zavod za statistika, 1994).

46. Historical evidence supports the latter, not the former, contention. See Niyazi Limanovski, *Islamizacijata i etničkite promeni vo Makedonija* (Skopje:

Makedonska kniga, 1993). Also see Katherine Verdery, "Ethnic relations, economies of shortage, and the transition in Eastern Europe," in C.M. Hahn, ed., *Socialism, Ideals, Ideologies and Local Practice*, (London: Routledge, 1993), pp. 172–86.

47. The precipitous banning of the Muslim veil (*zar* and *feredže*) in the early 1950s also created significant alienation of some Macedonian-speaking Muslims from the state and increased their sense that Macedonian identity was a Christian identity. The current dispute is thus not a new one; see Victor Friedman, "Language Policy and Language Behavior in Macedonia: Background and Current Events," in Eran Fraenkel and Christina Kramer, eds., *Language Contact, Language Conflict* (New York: Peter Lang, 1993), pp. 88–89. However, there are also Macedonian Muslim organizations actively encouraging Macedonian Muslim identification with Macedonian language and ethnicity.

48. *Nova Makedonija*, May 13, 1991; see also Friedman, "Language Policy."

49. An example of how "national" feelings in Macedonia are more complex than portrayed by ethnopolitical (or international) organizations is the Serbian husband of a Macedonian who, unbeknownst to his wife, had always declared himself a Yugoslav in national censuses. He went through a great personal crisis in connection with the 1994 census, because he did not wish to identify with current Serbian policies and did not consider Yugoslav to be a valid category any longer. He chose to declare himself as a Macedonian.

50. See Gal, "Diversity and Contestation in Linguistic Ideologies," pp. 344–45.

51. See Eran Fraenkel, "Urban Muslim Identity in Macedonia: The Interplay of Ottomanism and Multilingual Nationalism," in Fraenkel and Kramer, eds., *Language Contact, Language Conflict*.

52. See Stavro Skendi, *The Albanian National Awakening: 1878–1912* (Princeton: Princeton University, 1968), pp. 203, 207, 253.

53. The problem of identity in relation to both the census and Macedonian foreign relations received the following expression in the satirical journal *Osten*, July 8, 1995: "I'm going to declare myself as a Martian in the census." "Can you speak Martian?" "No need to. Here you can declare yourself a Turk or Albanian without knowing Turkish or Albanian. It's enough to be a Muslim. And as a Martian, no one can negate me. The Martians were never Greeks or involved in a Serbo-Bulgarian quarrel." "I dig it, buddy. You'll go far in life" (my translation).

54. *Flaka e vëllazërimit*, June 28, 1994.

55. *MILS*, January 26, 1995.

56. *MILS*, February 3, 1995.

57. Todorova, *The Balkans*, pp. 453–54.

58. Konrad Bercovici, *The Incredible Balkans* (New York: G. P. Putnam, 1932). Todorova has corrected this in her subsequent work.

59. One such feature is the replacement of infinitives by subjunctive clauses.

60. See note 5.

61. Personal notes dated July 1, 1994.

62. *MILS*, September 21, 1995.

63. Because no one in the mission speaks Turkish or Macedonian, it is not clear how they could judge the children's ability. See note 47.

64. See note 46 and the paragraph to which it refers.

65. A Greek colleague of mine who was born in 1950 told me that when he was growing up, people routinely referred to Western Europe as "Europe." For example, one might say, "I'm going to Europe for my vacation," as if Greece were not part of that entity.

66. Aleko Konstantinov, *Baj Ganjo* (Sofia: Daskalov, 1895).

67. The image of political Europe as a political or cultural entity that represents a desired or rejected "other" has been and is widespread in the economically peripheral nations of geographic Europe. See Susan Gal, "Bartok's Funeral: Representations of Europe in Hungarian Political Rhetoric," *American Ethnologist* 18, no. 3 (1991), pp. 440–58, for a Hungarian example of the same types of attitudes with additional references.

68. See Xhaferi, "Regjistrimi i jashtëzakonshem i popullsisë."

69. Susan L. Woodward, *Balkan Tragedy: Chaos and Dissolution After the Cold War* (Washington, DC: Brookings Institution, 1995), and Robert Hayden, (review of Woodward), *Slavic Review* 54, no. 11 (1995), pp. 14–15.

— INDEX —

Agani, Fehmi, 56
Ahrens, Geert-Hinrich, 89, 92, 93, 95, 100–101
Albania, 4, 82, 84; politics, 12, 17–18, 28, 78; relations, 12, 28, 75, 79–80; relations with Kosovo, 17, 33, 48, 75–78, 79–80; relations with Macedonia (Republic), 6, 17, 36–37, 38, 39, 40–41, 78–79, 120 n. 19; relations with Yugoslavia, 30
Albanians, 5, 75, 82, 120 n. 19; culture, 8, 21, 58–59, 78, 79; goals, 12, 20–21, 29, 31, 33, 51, 53, 56, 61, 76
Albanians in Kosovo, 49; education, 58–60, 69; politics, 3–4, 8, 27, 30, 47, 52, 57–58, 75–76
Albanians in Macedonia (Republic), 4, 34–35, 48–49, 79, 100–101, 102; education, 20–22, 32–33, 40–42, 63–64, 66–70; employment, 22–23, 61, 73; politics, 12, 23–24, 42–44, 60–63, 64–66, 71–75, 104; population, 88, 89, 92, 95, 96–97, 100

Aliti, Abdurrahman, 73–74, 94
Andov, Stojan, 23, 72
Arbnori, Pjeter, 77
Autonomy. *See* Territorial autonomy

Balkans, 3, 27, 81–82, 84, 99, 101, 103–5; recommendations for, 8–9; relations, 28; regional strategy for, 12; *See also* Albania; Bosnia-Herzegovina; Federal Republic if Yugoslavia; Kosovo; Macedonia (Republic)
Belgium, 38
Belic, Aleksandar, 87
Berisha, Sali, 18, 48, 78
Bexheti, Abdylmenat, 61
Borders, 18, 30; of Albania, 4; closing, 37, 38, 39; of Kosovo, 78; of Macedonia (Republic), 27, 33, 36, 40, 118 n. 3; *See also* Territorial claims; Territorial integrity
Bosnia-Herzegovina, 3, 33, 34, 36, 40, 51, 55, 78
Bosniac (census category), 89, 96
Boutros-Ghali, Boutros, 40